THAT TIME
I DIED

**AN EXTRAORDINARY JOURNEY
BEYOND THE VEIL OF LIFE AND DEATH**

From Death to Life to Healing

THAT TIME
I DIED

AN EXTRAORDINARY JOURNEY
BEYOND THE VEIL OF LIFE AND DEATH

Thomas Gates

ABBOTT
LANE
PUBLISHING

Published by Abbott Lane Publishing
Fayetteville, Arkansas
thomasgates.com

LCCN: 2024905298
ISBN: 979-8-218-36224-9 (paperback)
ISBN: 979-8-218-36225-6 (hardback)
ISBN: 979-8-218-36226-3 (ebook)

Available in paperback, hardback, and e-book

Any Internet addresses (websites, blogs, etc.) and telephone numbers printed in this book are offered as a resource. They are not intended in any way to be or imply an endorsement by Abbott Lane Publishing, nor does Abbott Lane Publishing vouch for the content of these sites and numbers for the life of this book.

DEDICATION

D EDICATED TO AND IN memory of my late parents, Henry and Bobbie Jo Gates, who innocently guided me towards my own spiritual path simply by the example of how they lived and loved in life. They were always there for me in good times and in challenging times. Their nurturing love and support were instrumental in helping me heal and reintegrate into this world as they encouraged me to joyfully embrace my new reality.

Contents

EPIGRAPH

"... the moment I realized that I was leaving my body, I had what would be the first of a few simple choices that occasionally presented themselves to me as my journey continued. This first choice was either to resist and fight what was happening or to simply let go and trust that everything would be all right. I chose to surrender to the experience of what was naturally unfolding. This was an easy choice to make because I was both physically and emotionally exhausted and I could not bear the thought of having to endure any more pain. Besides, it was a fascinating experience that now seemed to have a life of its own. Once I surrendered, I was no longer concerned with looking at the increasingly empty shell that my body was becoming. There was no fear or panic at all—just an ever-expanding sense of peace." But how did I get to this point? Well, let's start at the beginning...

INTRODUCTION

WHY I WROTE THIS BOOK

"WHAT? YET ANOTHER BOOK on the subject of Near-Death Experience? Aren't there enough already? I mean, what more could there possibly be to say about it?" That was my first response many years ago after sharing my story with a gathering of friends when they declared, "Oh, you have to write a book!"

Prior to that, I recall having seen bookstore shelves filled with various titles on the subject. I had never read one before at that early point in time because I assumed that surely this topic must have been covered quite thoroughly by now. What more could there be to add? Yet, more and more NDE titles kept appearing. So, it seemed there was a genuine interest to know more about this uncommon experience. After asking the aforementioned questions, I then asked why they insisted that I publish my story. Their answer was, "There is something in your story that we haven't heard before and we think it's really important for people to hear it." I often got this same response as I continued to share my experience in other group settings, which ultimately led me to finally say, "Well, ok then. It looks like I'm going to write a book!"

However, I wasn't initially sure exactly where to begin. This was a highly intimate and personal experience that I felt needed to be presented in a simple and uncomplicated way that would be accessible to people from all walks of life. But I knew one thing for certain that would simplify the process and fulfill that goal. When I just verbally shared the story, people always seemed to have some positive and often even cathartic responses. Aside from bringing some value of comfort and peace regarding the whole subject of death, it always seemed to bring about a natural and spontaneous release of some old deep-seated fears that had been with them for a very long time. So, I chose to write the story in the same way I had always shared it in those casual settings with friends. That seemed to be the most natural way of writing so that anyone who reads this book may possibly experience it as profoundly as those who have heard my story directly from me, in my own voice.

During my writing process, I was always aware that there are many other NDE stories and that there is not one "right" way to have such an experience. There are often some similar events that many NDEs seem to have in common: viewing the body from just above, being greeted by previously deceased loved ones, seeing a brilliant light, and more. But each and every journey will be different from one another. This is my story that is unique to me. Every NDE is also unique and perfect as it unfolds for each individual. Above all, I believe that Near-Death Experiences teach us more about life than death.

Now, after many years of starting and stopping, often setting aside my writing while I waited for words to come that could most clearly and precisely describe something that is almost beyond description, I can finally share my full story. It includes the events leading up to the NDE, the journey itself, the return to the body, the resulting dramatic changes it brought into my life, and some special healing gifts that spontaneously emerged over time. While this is not a "How To" book, it is my intention to share my story with the hope that it will simply enliven the underlying memory of our true, divine and eternal nature that uniquely resides within all of us.

I have sincerely made the effort to fulfill the wishes of those many friends and others who have continually encouraged me to write this book. Of course, I have made sure to include that missing "something" they felt needed to be told; the most important "something" that all human beings should know about the underlying essential nature of our existence. And that it is possible to experience the full range of being and the infinite connection we all have to one another and to the eternal Source of our own existence and that of all creation.

And about that title...

While the title of this book may at first seem a bit irreverent to some, that is not the intention at all. Aside from witnessing my own death process, or what is referred to as "Near-Death Experience," I certainly have known the great sense of loss when a loved one passes from this worldly existence. After all, I am human, capable of experiencing the wide range of possible emotions we are all touched by throughout our lives.

The whole point is that death is not the end of us—not the end of consciousness, of the soul. Even though the body will perish, we live on because of that first breath of God Source that gave rise to consciousness and all the creation. It can never "not" exist in some way or another. That is the grace bestowed upon us. I hope that as you read my story, you may be comforted and inspired by a vision of possibility and hopefully always consider to be more loving, caring, and compassionate as we walk together in this vast and marvelous field of creation. Forever inseparable...

NOTE TO THE READER

I HAVE ATTEMPTED TO share my story, as much as possible, in the chronological order of the events as they unfolded in this journey. Therefore, even though there are occasional references to notes that share additional thoughts outside of the story timeline, I recommend that you wait to refer to those notes until after completing Part 1. Then proceed in the same manner with each subsequent Part. In this way, you can walk alongside me, moment by moment, through that time I died...and beyond.

PART 1: DEATH, LIFE, AND HEALING

CHAPTER 1

MOTHER NATURE'S GIFT

*"I was innocently learning, through quiet
observation, nature's simple but truly
important lessons that would most
powerfully serve me throughout my life."*

G ROWING UP IN CENTRAL Texas, I had the good fortune
to spend long periods of time playing alone and
wandering about in the woods and hillsides. I spent many
hours every day walking, playing, innocently observing
everything going on around me and sensing that nature
always knew just what to do at any given moment. It
was not complicated, and it all seemed to flow with a
natural rhythm. The animals moved about with an ease
and grace showing no signs of strain or effort. Even
the trees seemed to gently bend and sway in perfect
harmony with the ever-changing winds. Season after
season would pass and everything in nature always seemed
to adapt and change without any resistance. I felt an
unspoken connection to *Mother Nature*, as if I had been

graciously allowed to witness some, but never all, of her precious secrets. Although I did not realize it at that time, our relationship was one of teacher and student. I was innocently learning, through quiet observation, nature's simple but truly important lessons that would most powerfully serve me throughout my life.

Along with my frequent adventures into the countryside, I also made time for many other childhood activities such as bicycling, baseball, water sports, and of course, school. My real passion, though, was drumming! My older brother played drums throughout his high school years, so there was always plenty of music around our home. Just as I had quietly observed the graceful, but deliberate movements of the animals, I watched my older brother's every move as he joyfully and effortlessly played his drums.

Then one day, at the age of nine, I finally decided that it was time for me to be a drummer, too. So, I sat down at my brother's drums and began to play. To my surprise and delight, I was immediately able to play basic rhythmic patterns or "grooves," as my brother, Jimmy, called them. That was it! I was hooked. I knew right then and there what I wanted to do for the rest of my life!

Jimmy began taking me to some of his rehearsals and performances, in addition to teaching me how to play as many musical styles as possible—everything from Blues, Big Band, Jazz and Dixieland to Country, Rock and Roll, and my all-time favorite—Soul Music. Within three years, I began playing professionally with various musicians, often at small private clubs and parties, county and state fairs, high school dances, and the occasional live holiday radio broadcasts.

I remember my very first "professional" gig in the summer of 1962, at the early age of twelve. My brother's group, with the requisite Elvis look-alike lead singer, was scheduled to play at a local roller rink sock-hop. However, Jimmy woke up that morning with a bad case of the flu, which got even worse as the day went on. By the time he should have been getting ready for the gig, he couldn't even get out of bed. He looked at me and mumbled, "You'll have to play the gig for me." My first response was, "What? I've never played a gig before!" To which he replied, "You can do it! You're ready." I trusted in my brother's judgment, and if he thought I was ready, then I believed I *was* ready!

Fortunately, I had never heard of the term, "stage fright." I was just so excited about getting to play that it never dawned on me I should or could be nervous. After setting up the drums and before the first song, the band leader turned to me and said, "Just keep it simple and steady and you'll be alright." 1-2-3-4... and away we went!

It all went amazingly well and was so much fun that I was both elated and sorry when it was over. I didn't want to stop! But then something interesting happened that got me even more excited about playing. The band leader came up to me and handed me $25. I said to him, "What's that for?" He told me that was my cut of the pay. I was astonished! "You mean to tell me that I get to have all this fun *and* get paid for doing it?" Now I *really* knew this is what I wanted to do!

Playing drums was effortless for me and I believe this was simply due, in large part, to my daily experience of witnessing and applying nature's constant lessons of non-resistance. I soon realized that the level of joy I experienced while playing drums was directly related to how easily my own body adapted to and blended with the drums' physical responses to being played. The depth of joy during this magical interaction was truly immeasurable.

CHAPTER 2

PERCEPTION: WHAT'S NORMAL ANYWAY?

"In those precious moments, I was graciously allowed to witness an expanded vision of this incredible earthly creation."

I N 1970, AT THE age of twenty, I decided to move to the Dallas-Fort Worth area, where I began to play drums in various dance halls, nightclubs, and bars. This was a new environment for me, where night after night I observed a different kind of nature: *Human Nature*, which I had always thought to be much more complex and not always so graceful and natural. Or so it seemed at the time....

During the next year, I developed a few close friendships with some of my fellow musicians and especially with some of the people who worked in the clubs. We were all members of a small, very close-knit family who cared for and watched over one another. So, when I discovered that many of my new friends had spent very little time, if any, in the countryside, I wanted to do something about that. In a way, I felt that perhaps they had missed out on something special by not growing up with the beauty of the woods in their lives, like I had. Of course, they probably felt that I had missed out on a lot by not growing up in the *Big City*. But in fact, I was finding city life to be quite intimidating at times.

One day I invited them all to come with me to visit the area where I had spent so many years of my life. I had not been able to go back there for a while, so it was, quite literally, like a breath of fresh air to leave the city and return to my roots.

A Magical Spiritual Experience

After giving my friends a brief tour of the woods, I decided to wander off on my own as I had often done as a child. I immediately fell into a deep, peaceful state of mind that, once again, opened me up to that exquisite stillness I had often felt in my childhood when I was alone in the woods. The initial cacophony of nature's various individual sounds began to seamlessly flow in perfect harmony. As I gazed up into the trees, the light was refracting after a recent rainfall, magically illuminating all the leaves and branches. Then, settling even more deeply into this incredibly refined vision, I was able to see something I had never seen before: subtler layers of the leaves and the life flowing through the veins that fed and sustained them. I could see just beneath the outer skin and deeper into the fabric that made up the density of the leaves, deeper and deeper, until I saw the smallest of cells collectively functioning and ultimately being expressed as the final shape and form of the leaves.

This gently unfolding vision began to spread into the surrounding branches and trunks of the trees. I saw a spider's web that had trapped several tiny, glistening beads of moisture. It was as if the beads and the strands of the web were one, completely inseparable, yet maintaining their own uniquely expressed form. I realized in those moments that everything was appearing as it truly is—not just in the seemingly limited, almost one-dimensional and isolated way that it usually appears. There was a faintly perceptible underlying essence that flowed through it all and gave it life. In those precious moments, I was graciously allowed to witness an expanded vision of this incredible earthly creation. I was deeply moved and felt honored to have been able to observe this amazing reality.

More, please...

When I finally left that area of the woods, my perception slowly began to fade back to the usual experience I had always thought of as *normal.* Only now, I knew that the old normal would never seem quite so normal again! This was such a powerful experience and I thought to myself, "There must be a way to experience this reality more than just on a rare and serendipitous occasion. Why not all the time?" My only problem was that I didn't have a clue as to how to go about achieving that.

I didn't feel that any of my previous academic or religious education had truly prepared me for such a profound "spiritual" experience. As a graduate of the Catholic school system, I surely must have participated in various discussions on religion and spirituality—but no one ever mentioned anything like this. And even though, admittedly, I was not a very good student in my religion class, I think I would have remembered something like this being discussed! It didn't necessarily seem to conflict with my traditional religious training, but it was just simply beyond the boundaries of what I had been taught: It's important to acknowledge God's presence, be prayerful, be compassionate and kind towards others, and even in some way be in the service of God. Of course, I always thought that one of the first and best things anyone ever told me about God was when I was just a child: "God is in everything. He's in the trees, in the plants, in the animals, and everywhere." Now *that* made sense to me! (Again, during my early childhood experiences in the woods, I had always sensed some invisible but powerful underlying essence that connected and permeated the various expressions of nature.) But from that point on, well, that's when it got more and more complicated. There were certain religious rules and regulations to follow that ideally could eventually lead one to an infinite space and time of eternal peace and joy. Or not... There was always the possibility of "Door Number 2" with an eternal outcome, as well! Either way, this was all expressed in terms of a *final* reward, at the end of one's life. However, during these few magical moments alone in the woods, I experienced an unbounded sense of timelessness, oneness, and a depth of peace and joy, unattached to and far exceeding any prior beliefs or expectations. And of course, I lived to tell about it! Life would go on, even though I had no idea of the incredible challenges I would soon be faced with.

The memory of this unusual experience was never far from my mind, and I was left with a haunting sense that I would never be able to quietly walk away from it. Once it happened, regardless of its unforeseen impending inconvenience or imposition on my life, or anyone else's for that matter, I could never pretend that it didn't happen and just go back to the way it was before. There was no going back!

CHAPTER 3

A SPIRITUAL QUEST BEGINS

"I knew that somehow, in its own time and its own way, the answer to my quest would have to come from a source of stillness somewhere deep within."

U PON MY RETURN TO the city, everything was different. Nothing seemed quite the same anymore. I became more restless with a steadily growing desire to seek out the meaning and the source of my remarkably sublime experience in the woods, one that I imagined should be available not just to me, but to all human beings. "What is this underlying silent source that permeates everything? Why are we not always clearly experiencing it in our lives? Is that even possible? If so, what more can we do to experience it now and always?" I wanted some answers! The next and most practical question was, "How and where do I begin?" The answer to that simple but most challenging question was not so obvious to me. I only knew that I could never turn away from pursuing it.

After a while, I began to feel more and more isolated, as many of my friends were finding it increasingly difficult to relate to me and my unwavering determination to follow this seemingly unconventional path, wherever it was leading me. There really wasn't any stressful conflict or confrontation over any of this. It's just that our common interests seemed to be heading in different directions. Even my wife at that time wanted to be supportive but was struggling to understand this new path I was pursuing, and she became more distant as time went on. Everyone wanted me to be the same old happy, easy going "TJ" that they had always been very comfortable with; but I was changing, and they didn't understand what was happening to me. Of course, *I* didn't really understand what was happening! All I knew was that I was probably never going to be satisfied with anything less than the full realization of my quest.

Searching

I began to look into some of the local spiritual groups and organizations that were following the more mystic, eastern traditions, hoping that there I might find what I was seeking. It appeared that the practices and beliefs of these traditions were bringing a certain level of peace and happiness to their followers. Even so, I was not ultimately inclined to join any of these groups. I simply didn't want to be bound by yet another limiting paradigm or have to adhere to any new dogmatic or compulsory belief systems that might potentially present more obstacles, rather than a natural pathway to the fulfillment of my deepest intention. Although I continued to search for the answer, I knew that somehow, in its own time and its own way, the answer would have to come from a source of stillness somewhere deep within.

CHAPTER 4

FROM TRAGEDY TO HOPE

I CONTINUED TO PLAY drums, but the city became increasingly dangerous, plagued by drug and gang related crime, as well as a heightened sense of racial tension. There were often sudden outbreaks of violence at some of the venues where I performed.

One particular evening, a gang fight started outside our club and people began to fight inside. As the chairs were flying and glass was breaking, a young woman lay on the floor suffering from a knife wound. The chaos turned into a full-blown riot and tragically, outside in the parking lot, a police officer was shot and killed.

After this shocking event, the stress and strain of living in such an environment took its toll. My health suffered as I became increasingly depressed and even more isolated from my friends. It was difficult to relate to this whole scene anymore and I longed for the peace and silence I had known in my childhood. I spent the next two years searching and hoping to find an answer. I began to wonder if I would ever find it and I continued to sink further and further into a deepening depression.

Renewed Hope and a Fresh Start

My older sister, Barbara, was living in Austin, Texas, where she had been practicing a special meditation technique for the previous two years. We didn't see each other very often during that time but, whenever we did, she always encouraged me to consider learning this method. She knew I was struggling in my life at that time, but she also knew that I was quite stubborn. I had continually resisted the idea of joining her in the meditation practice because I mistakenly assumed it meant having to join a group like the ones I had previously looked into. I felt, whether right or wrong, that what I was looking for would not come through any structured group, religion, or other organized belief systems, but it would have to come from the inside out—somewhere deep from within.

Over time, I had to acknowledge a gradual and steady change in my sister's life that seemed to bring her greater happiness and fulfillment. I was finally convinced by her progress and sincerity, along with her assurances that this was, indeed, a simple technique that I could practice without having to adopt any special religious or philosophical dogma to experience its benefits.

On February 27, 1972, I finally made the trip to Austin to visit my sister and learn how to meditate. During my initiation ceremony, I stood before a simple but neatly organized setting, complete with incense, a new white handkerchief, a couple of fresh oranges, bananas, and some flowers I had been asked to bring for this special occasion. There were a few other small ceremonial artifacts, including a framed picture of a revered holy man, whom I understood to be a late teacher from India whose intention it was for this ancient meditation technique to be brought into the modern-day world to help bring greater peace and enlightenment.

I was a little uncomfortable with this ritual at first, as it reminded me of my obstinate resistance to participate in such things. I soon let go of any discomfort when my instructor finally pronounced a *mantra* (a meaningless sound) which he asked me to softly repeat and then just think it silently. As soon as I followed this instruction, after only a couple of repetitions, I immediately slipped into a very deep level of silence. Even the mantra disappeared. It was such a peaceful silence that I don't at all recall being led down a hallway and into another room to sit in a chair and continue meditating. When someone eventually spoke to me to let me know it was time to end my meditation session, I had no idea how long I had been sitting there. When I slowly opened my eyes, only then did I realize that I was in another room—not the same room where I had started!

As I looked around, there was a rich quality of silence that permeated everything in the room—the walls, the chairs, the lamps, the paintings, the fireplace. Everything was uniquely expressed in shape and form, yet somehow seamlessly connected by an invisible, underlying essence. I felt an inseparable connection to everything in sight.

With a great sigh of relief, I thought to myself, "Ah... This is it!" I felt that this could be the key to unlock that invisible barrier between my ordinary perception and the subtle reality of the creation around me, just as I had experienced two years earlier while walking alone in the woods. What I had been longing for suddenly seemed to be truly possible to achieve. Immediately, my life seemed to be moving once again in a new and exciting direction. I felt a deep and fulfilling peace like I had not known for quite some time, and I was filled with hope and inspiration.

After a few days of enjoying this renewed peaceful state of mind, I just couldn't bring myself to go back to living and playing music in the city anymore. I was done with that stressful environment and wanted to make a new start somewhere else. So, I went to visit my parents, who lived in a small town near a lake a couple of hours outside of Fort Worth, Texas. They owned two homes there on a beautiful lake, surrounded by hundreds of acres of wooded countryside. While I was there, I decided to look for a job—a *regular* job that didn't have anything to do with bars and nightclubs or the potential for sudden outbreaks of violence. I wanted a clean break from all that.

I had always played drums to make my living, so I didn't really have many skills outside of that; but I found someone willing to give me a starting job at a manufacturing company in a nearby town. I was a little nervous about walking into something I didn't know anything about. Nevertheless, I was still excited about a fresh start—one that promised to be far removed from the struggles I had experienced for the past two years. I decided that I would get settled into the new job and then arrange for my wife to come join me. In the meantime, I was enjoying the blissful peace and silence of my daily meditation program. Everything was looking up and I was feeling more hopeful and positive about my life once again.

CHAPTER 5

EMERGENCY

*"Little did I know that my life
was about to change forever...."*

T HIS EUPHORIA LASTED FOR only a very short time when
I suddenly found myself being rushed to the hospital
with a case of acute appendicitis. I had been getting sick
during the weeks before, but I believed this was caused
by some recurring virus that I just couldn't shake. So,
one afternoon when I began to feel an occasional sharp
stabbing pain in my abdomen, I was not that concerned
about it. I thought it was just another flare-up from the
virus. Later that evening, as the pain increased both in
frequency and intensity, I realized this was something a bit
more serious than just a viral infection. I mentioned this
to my father, telling him, "I think I might have a case of
appendicitis. I don't really know much about it, but you
might want to be ready to take me to the hospital if it gets
worse." Indeed, it got worse. I suddenly collapsed in pain
and called out to my father. Since he had also been trained
as a paramedic, he knew exactly what to do. There was no

time to waste! He quickly wrapped me in a blanket, carried me out the back door to his truck, and raced us off towards the hospital.[1] As we flew over the gravel roads that led to the main road into town, I remember telling him, "Daddy, please slow down. It's only a couple of miles. I'll be alright!" He didn't slow down.

Upon my arrival, the doctors made their initial diagnosis and confirmed that acute appendicitis was the source of my suffering. They told me, "Don't worry. It's just a routine surgical procedure. You'll be home in about three days if all goes well." Little did I know that my life was about to change forever....

Unexpected Complications

The doctors had hoped to wait until morning but decided to perform surgery right away. They were concerned the appendix might rupture, so they administered pre-op medication and rushed me into the operating room. At this point, I just felt I could only trust that the doctors knew what they were doing and since I was heavily sedated, I really didn't care!

As they rolled me into the operating room, I began to feel slightly cold, even with all the bright lights reflecting down from just above. The room had a cold metallic appearance. There was glistening stainless metal everywhere I looked—metal trays, tables, instruments, and other unfamiliar hospital equipment. I felt like I was participating in a biology lab project but that *I* was the project! Suddenly, I became very anxious, and I really didn't want to do this anymore. But I thought to myself, "Oh well, there's not a lot I can do about it now." Trust...Trust...Trust.

There was a brief moment of levity, at least for the surgeons. One of them said, "Oh, he looks like he's already about to go under." I heard that and I thought they were going to start operating on me right away! I mumbled, "Hey, wait a minute! I'm still awake!" One of the doctors just laughed and said, "Well, don't worry. You won't be for long. Start counting backwards from ten." I dutifully began the countdown thinking, "I'll show him. I'll count all the way down to one and then we'll see what he has to say!" I began the countdown: "Ten, nine..."

I fought hard to hold onto my consciousness, but the floor was pulled out from under me. I was in a free fall and could do nothing to stop it. In a moment there was nothing. Not only was there no awareness—there was no sense of any existence at all! It was simply a black hole. *I* was just gone.

When I finally regained consciousness, I desperately wanted to escape and immediately return to that black hole again. The pain was more intense than any pain I had ever experienced in my life. It was unbearable and I had no idea what had just happened to me. I began thrashing about, like a wounded animal, trying to pull away the wires and tubes that had been attached to my body. It was like a terrible nightmare—only it was not a dream. It was a terrifying, inescapable reality! Finally, it took five strong nurses to hold me down while one administered the injection that quickly and mercifully returned me again to the sanctuary of that painless, empty black hole.

This state of drug-induced unconsciousness was nothing like sleep. It was a complete and total void. There were no thoughts, no dreams, and absolutely no sense even of my own being. I only realized that there had been a void as the drugs began to wear off and some faint awareness returned.

Every time I regained consciousness the pain raged throughout my body and pushed me beyond any reasonable ability to cope. This cycle continued for approximately four days until the potency of the pain-killing medication could gradually be reduced. As much as I dreaded the pain, I also hated the sensation of falling into that empty space of complete nothingness. Besides, there was apparently some concern about the possibility of my becoming addicted to the powerful narcotics. So, my willingness to tolerate the pain gradually increased as the medication was slowly, but steadily, reduced.

But all was not well. Someone tried to explain what had happened and why I was not, after all, going home after a quick and simple appendectomy. There were unexpected complications. During surgery the doctors found an alarming amount of inflammation throughout the intestines. Due to the severity of inflammation they quickly decided to explore a more expanded area to determine its source. This required a much deeper and lengthy incision in the abdominal area. What was initially expected to be a relatively simple and short operation, extended into a critical nine-hour procedure.

The circumstances under which the surgery was performed were not ideal. First, the doctors discovered something they were not expecting: a massive tumor in my colon. They had no idea at the time if it was malignant or benign, so it had to be dealt with immediately. There was no turning back. Then, since the tumor had caused a blockage in the colon, there was contamination when the tumor and additional inflamed areas of the colon were removed. This increased the risk of infection and the doctors had to continuously flood my body with antibiotics. If an infection developed that was not kept under control, then there could be a very serious threat to my life. As it turned out, their concerns later proved to be well founded.

No Visitors, Please!

Two of my good friends came to see me a few days following the surgery. This was the worst time to have visitors because of the difficulty I had coping with the pain and the additional irritation caused by the friction of a long tube that was inserted through one of my nostrils. The tube was attached to a pump to remove the excess fluids which had developed as a result of the surgery. I was encouraged to cough as much as possible to help keep the fluids moving but I was not particularly interested in doing this because it was very painful to do so. At times it felt like someone had literally started a fire in the lower half of my body. Occasionally, due to my reluctance to cough, the tube became blocked, and the nurse had to partially remove and reinsert it so the pump would continue to function. This procedure brought out the worst in me, as unfortunately witnessed by my visiting friends.

I saw the look in their eyes when they first entered the room. They were not prepared for what they were about to see and were obviously very uncomfortable. Then, to make matters worse, I began a coughing episode with its accompanying pain. This was just too much for them and I had to ask them to leave. After this experience I said to my father, "Please, don't let anyone else come to see me now." I didn't have the energy to spend on anyone else and I needed to focus all my attention on getting through the immediate crisis. Having others visibly upset by my appearance was even more unsettling to me.

CHAPTER 6

FIGHTING FOR MY LIFE

"...there was nothing else in the world except
for the battle being waged in my body."

A FEW DAYS HAD passed, and I seemed to be getting weaker and more agitated. My lungs began to fill more rapidly with fluid, and it was becoming increasingly difficult to breathe. The nurses continually encouraged me to cough as often as possible to help break up the congestion, but it was so painful that I soon gave up trying anymore. It became difficult to focus on anything other than the pain, as the fire in the middle of my body intensified with each passing moment.

It seemed that there was nothing else in the world except for the battle being waged in my body; it was simply about survival and there was very little energy left to be concerned about anything or anyone else. I began to withdraw in a more inward direction, and I sensed that no one else could help me now. I, alone, would have to find the will to survive this incredible challenge.

Sometimes, when the pain briefly diminished, I realized there had been gaps of time that I could not account for. (Only many years later I remembered, in a very dramatic way, significant events that had happened during those gaps.)[2]

There were also moments when I became aware of others in the room and could very clearly hear them speaking. It was odd because they were not speaking to me, as if I couldn't hear them anyway. But I could! I wanted to speak, but I couldn't! Why weren't they aware that I could hear them? Those were very disconcerting moments for me because it was as if I didn't seem to matter anymore.

But of course, I did matter. I mattered to my father who had been sitting in that hospital room since I first came out of surgery. He was right there through it all, always silently giving his love even when I could not see, speak, or hear. His presence was very strong, and his love proved to be even more vast and powerful as I moved into deeper levels of my experience.

Gaps In Time

The gaps in time became more frequent as I drifted from awareness of the pain into some deep, silent space while my body fought its battle. At one point, after a brief period of silence, I very clearly experienced being in the middle of what appeared to be a train wreck. In the dark of the night, I saw twisted metal, steam, flashing lights, fire and smoke all around me. I heard voices moaning and crying out for help. Looking down to see what was causing the hot burning fire in the middle of my body, I saw a long, narrow piece of metal almost cutting me in half. It all seemed so real and, in fact, years later would reveal and heal a particular fear very much related to this frightening moment.[3]

After this experience, I was back on hold again as my body continued its struggle to survive. As I was just emerging from one of those quiet and painless moments, a spinning wheel suddenly came into view. Occasionally it stopped and a benevolent face appeared, smiling and speaking tenderly to remind me that I was loved. Then, the wheel would start to spin again and then stop with another face appearing. This happened over and over. They were all older women who, at first, seemed vaguely familiar until I suddenly realized who they were. They were family members from past generations of long ago who were there to help me stay in a simple space of surrender.

More Gaps

CHAPTER 7

LEAVING THE BODY

"It was true. I was dying. I was slowly, but most certainly, emptying out of my body."

BY THIS TIME, MY condition had severely deteriorated. I had become incredibly weakened as the systemic infection continued to spread throughout my body. The doctors and nurses grew increasingly concerned about the impending threat of organ failure, due to a seemingly unstoppable infection and a dangerously high fever. This led to the decision to surround my body with cooling packs to reduce my body's temperature and, for a time, it seemed to have a positive effect and temporarily lowered the fever somewhat. At this point, the nurses seemed confident enough to leave the room for a short while. However, the high temperature soon returned and once again soared to a dangerous level.

In the midst of this chaos, I suddenly heard someone walk into the room and say to my father, "We're sorry. We've done everything we can. We're not sure he's going to make it." Then the person quietly walked out of the room. I heard the words, but I could not even begin to believe them. I could not move or speak but I remember shouting inside my head, "That's crazy! You're in the wrong room! There's no way I'm going to die! I'm too young to die!" It just seemed totally impossible to me that I could actually die. It was, in fact, the most absurd thing I had ever heard in my life! Within moments after silently declaring to myself that I was not going to die, something very strange began to happen. As my fever approached 107 degrees, all the pain suddenly and completely stopped! All the intense chaos I had endured for so long just vanished in an instant. I was very thankful for that, but I was not at all certain what was really happening. Then I began to feel an odd sensation stirring in my feet. It started in my toes and began to move very slowly farther up my feet, into my ankles, and into my legs. There was a sheet covering my body from my feet to my chest, yet I could see right through it as I looked at the areas wherever the sensation was occurring.

As I looked down, I saw only an empty shell in the shape of my feet—like a cicada's empty molted shell. I was captivated by this view as the process slowly continued to move up my legs and farther up into my body. Once it reached my chest, I finally realized what was happening. It was true. I *was* dying. I was slowly, but most certainly, emptying out of my body.

Choices

In that moment, I had what would be the first of a few simple choices that occasionally presented themselves to me as my journey continued. This first choice was either to resist and fight what was happening or to simply let go and trust that everything would be all right. I chose to surrender to the experience of what was naturally unfolding. This was an easy choice to make. I was both physically and emotionally exhausted and I could not bear the thought of having to endure any more pain. Besides, it was a fascinating experience that now seemed to have a life of its own. Once I surrendered, I was no longer concerned with looking at the increasingly empty shell that my body was becoming. There was no fear or panic at all—just an ever-expanding sense of peace.

This "emptying" process continued to move up past my chest, into my neck, my face, and into my head. Finally, I simply popped out of my body through a tiny spot at the very top of my head, just where it begins to curve downward at the crown, near the back of the head.[4]

Room With a View

I looked down below and saw my lifeless body lying on the bed. Although I saw it from just above, at first, I didn't recognize it. I thought, "What is that?" Then I realized, "Hey, that's me! But wait! How can that be me because I'm up here looking down at that?" That was the moment when I truly understood that nobody really dies. My body was still there but it was an empty box. A tiny box! I thought to myself, "How could I possibly have been contained in such a small space like that?" I was so much bigger than that! It was as if I had spent my entire life living in a tiny house and only now, as I was suddenly evicted, did I realize this. If I had gone no farther than this and then returned to my body, it would have been well worth the price of admission! It was worth any amount of suffering I had gone through to have this one amazing realization: Our bodies may die but we somehow continue to exist and to experience beyond its physical boundary.

Looking down into the room, I saw my father sitting quietly in a chair. I sensed that he didn't know what was happening to me at that moment. There was a perfect silence as I floated above the ceiling and the rooftop, rising farther and farther away from my body. It was like looking down on a dollhouse that had no roof. Everything kept getting smaller and smaller. As that view became less defined and more distant, I finally turned away from it and no longer felt any attachment to anything at all. It just didn't matter anymore. Soon, even the memory and any concept of the past or the future would completely disappear from my reality.

CHAPTER 8

LOVING BEINGS

"Don't worry, everything is alright. We love you. We're here to help you. We love you."

T HE SENSATION OF MOVEMENT stopped momentarily and there seemed to be *nothing*; just a vast, dark, empty space. I had no idea what might happen next and wondered, "Is there something in particular that I'm supposed to do now?" Since I didn't recall ever having done this before, I was once again faced with the choice of either being fearful or simply surrendering to the moment. The next event completely removed any possibility of fear or doubt throughout the rest of my journey.

Suddenly, five beings appeared before me. They all had a bright, glowing white luminescent appearance. Three of them were standing side by side. The other two were standing just in front and were slightly shorter than the others. I could clearly see their faces, but I didn't recognize them. Although they looked only slightly different from one another, the three in back had a very subtle masculine energy while the other two beings had a more feminine quality about them. This was not discernible in any way by their physical appearance, but only by a most refined projected essence.

The two beings in front directly communicated with me, without speaking, while the others looked on benevolently. It all happened within a deep, rich quality of silence but they very clearly and repeatedly expressed to me, "Don't worry, everything is alright. We love you. We're here to help you. We love you." Their presence was very soothing, and I clearly felt their unbounded love for me. In fact, I had never experienced such a depth of unbounded and reassuring love. No strings attached—just pure and simple but powerful love. They were there to help me understand that I was not alone, that I was loved, and that there was absolutely nothing to fear. I felt that I could let go and trust in the freedom of innocently and fully experiencing whatever may come, moment by moment, without any attachment, projection, or desire. What happened next completed this understanding and set the stage for an unencumbered journey into an almost infinite, expanding field of subtler and subtler layers of creation and beyond....

Dissolution

Sensing the presence of another being, I gradually turned my attention towards him. I instantly felt an even greater wave of peace and comfort wash over me as I recognized who he was. He was the late Swami Brahmanand Saraswati, often simply referred to as Guru Dev.[5] I had not thought of him at all since the day of my instruction in the meditation technique, but I remembered him from the picture I had seen a few days before during the meditation initiation ceremony. As he appeared to me in these moments, I knew there was absolutely nothing to fear. He did not speak, but only lovingly gazed upon me for some time. I knew that no words were necessary. His powerfully strong and loving presence gave me a sense of strength, trust, peace, and surrender to whatever may come next. Most importantly, I was absolutely and completely released from any attachment to the past. In fact, in those few precious moments, the past had disappeared along with any memory of what had ever come before, including any memory of the body or the world I had left behind.

Off the Clock

The stage was set. I was "off the clock," as all sense of time disappeared. With no past or future, I could now gracefully and fearlessly move through the unbounded journey that I was about to take. I was left with no possibility of limiting thoughts, beliefs, or expectations of what may come; just a simple freedom to fully experience each event only as it happened in its unique moment, and then being free of any binding memory of it ever having occurred. Moment by moment, without any judgments of right or wrong, good or bad, better or worse. Experience after experience—there was only one time: The Present.

CHAPTER 9

THE TUNNEL AND THE GOLDEN LIGHT

*"With a sudden euphoric exhilaration,
I entered into the light!"*

I SOON FELT A sensation of movement once again and began to enter a rapidly expanding tunnel. The walls of the tunnel were only a very subtle boundary that had a faint appearance, much like a veil. The outer edges, far off in the distance and barely perceptible, had a soft gauze-like texture. The tunnel was black, much like the black of night. At first, there was simply nothing to see, but then the blackness began to serve as a distinct contrast, or backdrop, for all the visions that began to appear as I gently moved through its space. I was expanding into all the space around me. The farther I moved through the tunnel, the farther the faint boundaries seemed to move away. I continually perceived something just beyond the veil, but whatever it was, it was not apparent to me and, therefore; it was of no concern.

The Thread

As I traveled through this space, I was faintly aware, only through a peripheral vision, of a soft and almost translucent pale blue cord that seemed to be floating along behind me. Only much later, after my journey was completed, did I realize that it went all the way back into the earthly existence I had just left behind and was connected directly to my father's heart. I believe the pure essence of his unwavering, unconditional love silently followed me throughout my journey and was instrumental in helping me later return to the still, forgotten body that lay before him.

After I became free of my body, I was never aware of having any shape or form throughout the entire experience. However, as I continued to move within this vastly expanding tunnel, I began to see thousands of beautiful, crystal-like blue glowing lights, some slowly ascending and others descending throughout the tunnel. They steadily moved in long columns that were dispersed all around. This was a stunningly beautiful vision, combined with a perfect silence. I later realized that I most likely had the same appearance. I understood that these were other souls that were making the transition either to or from their worldly bodies.

The Golden Light

Suddenly, the tunnel opened up as my awareness continued to move deeper into an ever-expanding, silent space. I had emerged from the tunnel and there was no longer any sense of even the faintest boundaries that had appeared before. As I gently moved along in that incredibly deep silence, a soft, glowing white light began to appear in the distance. There was only a fraction of a moment when I had a choice either to go to the light or turn away and continue in another possible direction. From the first moment I saw it, there was absolutely no hesitation. I was already on my way to the light![6]

It had a magnetic quality that gently drew me towards it. As I came closer and closer, the light began to change into a brilliant golden color which soon became my entire field of vision. With a sudden euphoric exhilaration, I entered into the light. I was immediately and completely absorbed by it; literally becoming one with this extraordinarily intense, yet peacefully soothing light that seemed to be endless. There was absolutely nothing but a pure golden brilliance, along with a faint sense of being embraced by a gentle healing essence.[7]

I suppose I might have just remained in this state forever but then, as easily as I had entered into it, I suddenly had passed through it and continued to move forward in my journey. There was no feeling of loss or sorrow about moving beyond the perfection of the light and into the next experience. Since there was no longer any past, there was no longer any memory. I could not become attached to any one experience. Again, it was simply impossible to make any judgments or comparisons about anything; therefore, each new moment could only be an expression of perfection.

CHAPTER 10

THRESHOLD TO THE SOURCE

"I had completely left the field of the created universe and melted back into the unmanifest Source of myself and that of all creation."

A FTER EMERGING FROM THE golden light, there was an expansive depth of pure silence. I was embraced by a warm, nourishing, and infinitely expanded space that had no boundaries. It was a perfect continuum of deepening silence; I experienced myself *only* as the silence itself. Occasionally, there were some very subtle, sparkling visual ripples, as if something was beginning to manifest into a denser, more fully expressed form; but it was hardly enough to shake me from the deep, peaceful state of silence.

Finally, as I gently emerged just beyond this ever so subtle experience, I had a sensation of moving into and through a vast space of darkness, once again. Although I could clearly perceive an almost infinite depth of darkness, there was nothing to see. There was no thought, concern, or fear and, therefore, no judgment about it. The darkness had no meaning. It was simply "what was" at that moment.

Suddenly, a very clear, pristine, geometric particle appeared. It was a stunning sight that was illuminated by an intense but invisible light source. The contrast between the darkness and the reflected brilliance enlivened the particle's remarkably precise detail. I was greatly enlivened by its very presence. It was made of eight clear, glass-like pyramids. Four standing in a square pattern with the edges of their bases almost touching but precisely spaced, with a very small gap between each of them. Then there was a mirror image of them immediately below standing with their bases directly facing the bases of the above four pyramids, yet not touching any of the others. This particle was rotating, turning, and spinning very slowly and gracefully, end over end. As it rotated, I could see the multiple edges appear as fine lines intersecting one another in a constantly changing, but orderly manner. The incredible precision of its design and movement was absolutely flawless.[8]

My observation of the particle finally ended and with it, so ended all the rest of perceptible creation. I had crossed an invisible threshold and was now just outside the field of any manifested physical existence. Here, there was nothing—not even the perception of "nothing." Since there was nothing created, there was nothing to perceive. Since there was nothing to perceive, there was no mechanism needed with which to perceive. It simply did not exist. I had completely left the field of the created universe and melted back into the unmanifest Source of myself and of all creation.[9]

There was no need, no desire, no thought, no expression, and no experience. There was no longer any concept of time and space. All time had ended—including the "present." Even my own individual sense of "self" had disappeared. I did not exist absolutely in any form that could be identified with the "me" that has experienced (or would ever experience) anything in *any* level of creation. There was nothing to know, to do, or to be. It was simply a state of unexpressed perfection, beyond even any possible definition of "perfection" as we know it. It was purely just an invisible, unmanifest Source with the potential to give rise to a manifesting creation and individual experience. There are no words that can truly describe this state because, again, it was and is beyond the field of experience and, therefore, truly beyond description.

CHAPTER 11

THE BIRTH OF CONSCIOUSNESS

*"The greatest gift of this extraordinary moment
was the realization that there was one
underlying Source of all creation and that I
was eternally inseparable from that Source."*

T HEN, IT WAS AS if somehow the "Breath of God" gently exhaled and miraculously propelled me back into an emerging existence, once again. I was beginning just at the edge of where that unmanifest Source becomes the very first and most subtle moment of creation. Then there was instantly a contrast through which I could give meaning to that which, just before, was beyond experience and meaning.

With the ability to perceive once again, through this amazing birth of consciousness, I could now look back towards an invisible space and realize where I had just been. Only then, as my own consciousness was (re)manifesting into creation, where I had seen the last but now first particle, did I understand the *nothingness* that was just beyond that invisible threshold. "*That* is what *I* am. *That* is the Source of my being." Then, as I turned towards the unfolding creation before me, I saw subtle particles rapidly beginning to take shape and form. I understood, "All *this* is *that*, too." And finally, "*I* am all *this* and *this* is all *that*. There is nothing that is not *that* Source and *of* that Source."

The greatest gift of this extraordinary moment was the realization that there was one essence, one underlying Source of all creation and that I was eternally inseparable from that Source, or from any other particle of the entire universe. Everything at any level of existence was born of and permeated by that Source essence.[10]

As more particles continued to appear and the creation began to expand, I had the faint thought, "Who is creating this experience?" Although there was still no sound to be heard, the silent, but explicit answer was immediate, "You are!" I realized that I could never truly know *how* consciousness had mysteriously manifested, but I now clearly knew *why*. Consciousness had instantaneously become the unifying thread that connected the experience of the wholeness of creation to its unmanifest Source. Nothing could happen without consciousness, born of the Source. And consciousness could not happen without the underlying impulse of Source to give rise to consciousness. It was the magical ingredient in those moments that could ultimately become the catalyst through which to perceive the unlimited manifest expressions of Source. That Source, which in its perfect unmanifest state in and of itself, has no expressed value. Then something had to become the instrument through which that Source could be known. I understood that was why I had become a conscious being. I was now a vehicle, in a sense, born of the silent Source through which there could be the experience, and thereby, the acknowledgment and appreciation of that underlying invisible Source.

Later, as my journey continued into a more densely compressed world, I would clearly realize that all this incredible variety of creation is by and for all of us, through the grace of that God Source from which we spring forth. The most fundamental questions of, "Who, What, When, Where, Why, and How am I?" were all instantly answered in the most wondrous moment I would ever know—this first moment of the birth and existence of consciousness.

None of this understanding came by way of any empirical thinking process. It was fully unveiled in the flash of a moment, with no analysis and no intellectual paradigm to ponder. I knew that I was playing a part in the creation of my reality but there was no forethought or planning as to what should, could, or would happen next. Once again, there was just the peaceful and perfect elegance of the present unfolding moment by moment.

CHAPTER 12

RETURN TO THE BODY!

*"I was suddenly slammed back into my body...
but I had absolutely no memory of who, what,
or where I was; no memory of ever having
been here before."*

WITH NO EXPERIENCE OR concept of any direction, distance, or destination, I began to have another sensation of movement; but now I was aware that there seemed to be no actual *space* anymore. Because of the continuum of the underlying wholeness and connection of that wholeness to myself and to all of creation, there was "no space for space." There was the appearance of subtly contrasting qualities of that oneness, as expressed throughout the ever-expanding variety of the unfolding creation. But there was no experience of separateness. The individual and universal threads of consciousness, the particles, and the eternal, invisible fabric of the creation, were all seamlessly woven together as one—all uniquely expressed, but completely inseparable. Each moment of the journey now led to only one continuously fulfilled destination: Wholeness.

Throughout my journey I had moved along at a very easy, peaceful, and comfortable pace, but now, as the accumulation and density of this physical matter was rapidly increasing, I began to have the sensation of moving much faster. I was no longer able to clearly distinguish the unique shapes and forms of the various particles as they appeared when suddenly, I was flying deeper and deeper into the thickness of a much more concentrated mass.

The expansive tunnel I had experienced after initially leaving my physical body was now replaced with a much more compressed and tightly closed, narrow tube-like tunnel. I was flying through it at an incredibly intense rate of speed. Shards of white, green, and black were flying past me in random and chaotic fashion. Finally, I could no longer distinguish any specific detail or form. Speeding back through an increasingly dense and seemingly chaotic time and space, spinning, winding, and turning, I was suddenly slammed back into my body with the powerful force like that of a wet cloth being thrown against a brick wall!

My head suddenly snapped back, and my eyes opened widely. I was staring at a flat white surface that had hundreds of small randomly spaced, glowing sculpted indentations which gradually came into focus—an object that I much later understood was simply a hospital room ceiling tile! For several moments, I just stared at it, not knowing what it was. As I slowly began to look around,

I realized that I was surrounded by a huge amount of very dense matter. There were walls, doorways, windows, instruments and machines, none of which I yet recognized. I saw something suddenly move and thought to myself, "What's that?" It was my own hand! I was in this body, but I had absolutely no memory of *any* of this. I didn't know where I was or who I was. I didn't even know *what* I was in this space and time.

Then, I saw a man sitting just a few feet away who had a look of both relief and concern. I felt a strong connection to him but, like everything else, I did not recognize him, either. Surprised by my own ability to speak, I asked, "What happened?" The man answered, "Don't you remember, son? You were very sick and had to have surgery. We thought we were going to lose you." I had no idea what any of that meant but when I heard the word "son," I realized, from the depth of some faint memory, that this man was my father. I just looked at him and said nothing. I somehow understood the concept, but I still didn't remember him. I had been so far removed from this realm of physical creation that I simply had no memory of ever having been here before.

The doctors, the nurses, and my father were all relieved that I had gotten through the physical crisis and that I was back from the brink of death. Only, I wasn't back yet; at least apparently, not quite the same as I had been before. I still did not remember. Now I had a body, but it wasn't at all clear to me exactly *why*.[11]

Unfamiliar Territory

Although I did not tell anyone, I was not at all concerned by the fact that I had no memory of this body or this place where I now found myself to be. I knew who I *really* was because only then, once I was back in the body, did I have the complete chronological memory of everything I had just experienced in my journey, including the true, essential nature of my existence. So, I simply continued to accept everything as it was in the moment. This worked just fine for me; however, I could see that it was not working particularly well for my father and the nurses who were there. They didn't directly or outwardly express any alarm about this. Perhaps they were afraid to say anything that might upset me in those delicate moments, but I could sense their concern. They kept gently trying to explain to me what had happened. Of course, they had no idea of what had *really* just happened to me! How could they possibly know?

After a while, I finally had my first memory of having been in this body before. It was terrifying! I remembered the pain—the agonizing pain. I braced myself for its return, gripping the side rails of the bed. I dreaded having to go through that again and for the first and last time since my return, I momentarily felt a deep sorrow for having to be in this body and in this world.[12] Having experienced such a beautiful, unbounded essence of myself, without the limiting restrictions of individual form, I wondered why I had to come back and experience the pain of this incredibly fragile body.

Then, something very interesting happened... nothing happened! The pain did not return. It was done. The crisis was over, and I could now begin a new journey of recovery. Oh, I certainly was not completely free of pain, by any means. Within a day or two, the doctors insisted that I be helped out of bed to slowly walk and straighten up as much as possible; thus, reducing the potential for developing internal adhesions and other related problems. Although this activity was extremely difficult and painful, it could never compare to the intense, unbearable pain I had endured in the battle for my life before my extraordinary journey had begun.

Within a couple of days other parts of my memory began to return. At first, I simply had to take some things on faith, but I soon began to recall a few simple memories. I remembered my father and mother, family and a few friends, and gradually, a few childhood experiences. Although they were slowly filtering in, I didn't feel any concern or urgency regarding my lack of memories. In fact, the past just didn't seem so important anymore and it was certainly less interesting than what was happening in the present moment.

Even with my slowly emerging memories, I knew that nothing would ever be the same again. I was different now. The reality of my own sense of existence had just been dramatically altered and, as I was lying there in that hospital bed, I really didn't have any idea what was about to unfold in my life.

CHAPTER 13

A TIME TO HEAL

"I was very weak, but I just knew that if I wanted to get well, this was not the place where it would happen."

S O, THERE I WAS, stuffed back into a tiny, weakened body which hardly seemed appropriate to contain the full reality of what I had just experienced myself to be. It was also abundantly clear to me that this body was not in very good condition. Although it was going to take time for it to heal and become stronger, I had no doubt that an even greater healing had already taken place. There was an inner strength that would carry me through and beyond the lengthy physical healing process I was about to begin.

For many years, I did not fully realize exactly why I had to be in this body, but I did not resist it. There were no regrets and there was no desire to leave it again any time soon. It was simply where I found myself to be. I knew that I must have chosen this life and this body for a very good purpose—a divine purpose that would perhaps someday be clearly revealed to me.

After having been in the hospital for nearly a month, I felt the need to leave there as soon as possible. I had primarily been sustained by massive amounts of antibiotics, intravenous saline solution, and, on occasion, even *Jell-O*. I had not been able to eat any solid food, so the first prepared food I received was a serving of over-cooked vegetables presented in pureed form. I had barely survived the surgery but now, I was not at all certain that I would survive eating from the hospital's menu. After all I had been through, it would have been tragic to perish from malnutrition!

The medical staff felt that I was too weak and that it was too soon for me to leave. I had already lost 45 pounds since first arriving at the hospital and now I barely weighed 100 pounds. Naturally, I was very weak, but I just knew that if I wanted to get well, this was *not* the place where it would happen. I also knew, with absolute certainty, that it was time to go and that everything would be alright. The doctors were legitimately concerned about my delicate condition and warned me that it would be very easy to injure myself or become ill again if I were not careful. I could end up right back in the hospital with more serious complications to deal with. After repeated assurances that I would be very careful, my persistence ultimately prevailed, and everyone finally agreed to my release.

New Light of Day

Since I didn't have the strength to walk out of the hospital on my own, I was gently helped into a wheelchair and rolled towards the main entrance. I was completely unprepared for what I experienced as I passed through the doors and into the sunlight. Everywhere I looked there was a lively, effervescent quality that seemed to permeate everything that lay before me. The sunlight, the sky, the sounds, the smells, the colors and, of course, many more wonderful human beings! It was all so incredibly clear and vibrant and connected. I was like a child in a candy store. Everything looked good! It was indeed good to be alive.

Even with the occasional uncomfortable bumps and bounces of the ride home from the hospital, a reminder of my mortal physical existence, I was glad to be alive in this world. From that moment on, I would have a very different and much broader appreciation for life. I knew that nothing would ever be the same, regardless of however it was before. It was as if one life had ended, and a new one had begun—an exciting journey into a new life. I realized that the true beginning of this life-journey was in that magical moment when I had witnessed the birth of consciousness from the unmanifest Source of all creation. Moreover, since I knew that my own eternal nature and every particle of creation is permeated and sustained by that unmanifest Source, my journey of life truly has no beginning or ending. And so it is for every human being.

Life is eternal... Nobody dies.

PART 2: A NEW LIFE JOURNEY

CHAPTER 14

LIFE 2.0

"I was now functioning within the boundaries of a very densely manifested human body surrounded by an even more densely manifested diversity, all of which made this new adventure quite fascinating."

AFTER LEAVING THE HOSPITAL, I initially returned to my parent's home to begin the lengthy process of recovery. It was obviously going to take some time to regain my strength before I could go out into this new world. There was some physical therapy to aid in the healing process, along with special dietary requirements to help me regain my strength. Even so, from the very day I returned to the body, there was no doubt whatsoever that it was on a path of healing. The crisis was over and now it was just a matter of time before my body would be strong and healthy once again. I was absolutely certain of that; however, I was not at all certain about the purpose of having returned to this physical life and what path it might take. I just took it one day at a time, trusting in this new adventure and especially enjoying being present to every precious moment.

Of course, my mother and father were incredibly happy that I had survived this crisis. They were more than willing to help nurture me back to good health with that special kind of loving care that parents instinctively know how to give to a child, no matter how old that child may be. I was very blessed to have them in my life, especially during such a vulnerable stage in my recovery.

During this time of convalescence, I soon became aware that my perception and experiences in this world were significantly different than what others around me seemed to experience. I was mostly just observing the events as they unfolded, without any overt emotional attachment to my own actions or the actions of others. There was a subtle, continual silence underlying and permeating, moment by moment, any activity I was involved in. Sometimes, it was very much like watching a movie on a big screen. I was actively engaged in my actions and yet, I was also the audience to my own experiences. This was not disorienting or disconcerting in any way; on the contrary, it generally seemed to be completely normal. In fact, it was a natural extension of how things had unfolded during my death experience. The significant difference being that I was now functioning within the boundaries of a very densely manifested human body surrounded by an even more densely manifested diversity, all of which made this new adventure quite fascinating.

Unbounded Boundaries

Even with the initial physical challenges, not to mention the significant gaps in my life's old memory banks, I never once regretted that I had returned to this body and this worldly life. Yes, I had experienced that incredibly expansive and unbounded nature of my own being only a few weeks before, but I never longed to go back to "the other side." I knew, without a doubt, that there is only *one* side—just differently expressed values of that eternal source throughout all creation, through me, and through everyone and everything, never separate. (*Much like the two sides of a coin: One side is Heads, and the other is Tails, seemingly different from each other. But turn the coin edgewise and see that there is something that bonds the two together. Not only that, but that "something" gives rise to, permeates, and unifies both sides, which are just differently expressed values of the underlying, unifying source from which their uniquely expressed values exist.*)

Based on that experience and understanding, it is possibly why in the early days, weeks, and months of my recovery, I sometimes found myself quite naturally and spontaneously, without any direct intention, easing in and out of the defined boundaries of my body. One such experience occurred shortly after being reminded that I had learned how to meditate and was given some instruction again about how to do that. I often meditated while sitting on the bed at my parents' guest house. But one day, as I sat meditating in a chair near a window in the living room, I became aware of a very fine, soft summer breeze gently moving the window's translucent gauze curtain. I felt the fresh air gently touching my face and noticed that the light outside seemed to have a vibrant, glistening quality. Everything I saw through the window was extraordinarily pristine and clearly defined, yet somehow softly inter-connected and inseparable, much like those initial moments after opening my eyes when I had first learned to meditate. And now, as before, I experienced a deep, profound sense of peace.

Then, at some point, I looked across the room and noticed that my body was actually sitting on the bed in a different windowless room. My awareness had somehow spontaneously migrated to the living room where my perception functioned as if I were sitting in the chair by the window. Having previously experienced this kind of "bilocation" phenomenon during my time at the hospital, I was not surprised or disturbed by it. So, after a few moments, I just naturally drifted back and began to experience perception from my physical body once again. I knew that I had not really ever left it. It's just that my sense of perception was not bound in those moments by the physicality and location of my body.

CHAPTER 15

THE ILLUSION OF SEPARATENESS

"I realized how our present reality can be so easily influenced and altered by our past—past beliefs and judgments, past memories and past fears—the illusion that costs us in our affinity for love."

I OFTEN FELT THAT subtle connection to my surroundings even outside of meditation. One early evening, I decided to take a short walk across the yard to my parents' house for dinner. I didn't bother to put on any shoes since it was not far to go. As I was about to step down off the patio onto the ground, I stopped and began to admire something there that had a richly patterned, colorful design. It was only inches away from where I was standing, and I was enthralled by its natural beauty. Then suddenly, some old memory from the past emerged and I literally jumped backwards through the air and landed about eight feet from where I had been standing. The beautiful object

I had been admiring was a large and highly poisonous copperhead snake! Just as I jumped back, the snake also jumped back in the opposite direction and made a fast get-away. This frightful moment was triggered by a sudden sense of separateness, ending a peaceful and graceful communion that had existed only moments before and, thus, opening the doorway to fear.

This was my first real experience of fear since shortly before my recent death experience. In fact, I never had any fear throughout the entire experience of dying and the subsequent journey I had taken. And now I was suddenly afraid of such a beautiful creature? Wow! One moment there was a peaceful, mutual connection devoid of any fear whatsoever and the next, we were both instantly repelled from each other.

I felt a brief sense of sadness in that moment as I realized how our present reality can be so easily influenced and altered by our past—past beliefs and judgments, past memories and past fears—and what it costs us in affinity for love and life. Soon after this experience, I witnessed an event that was even more shocking.

Immediately after leaving the hospital and returning to be cared for by my parents, I was sheltered from much of the outside world, at least in the beginning. This was initially because of my delicate physical condition but also because I needed a gentle "re-entry" while regaining more memory of this life. After a while, my mother occasionally invited some of the neighbors over to visit. I quickly remembered some of them but sometimes it was like meeting others for the first time. Of course, Mother always forewarned them about the "memory thing."

I recall one day when we were sitting around the back patio with a neighbor who lived just a few houses away. I didn't remember her, but she was, graciously, not bothered by that fact and I found her to be quite delightful. A little while later, a man, who turned out to be her husband, drove up and began angrily shouting at her about something she had said or done that was upsetting to him. His words were so rude and hurtful that her delightful demeanor of only a few moments before was suddenly crushed. I was quite shocked to witness this disturbing event. I still understood and experienced that we are all really of the same essence and that even though we are uniquely expressed in different ways with different personalities, preferences, and so on, we are all infinitely connected and inseparable. So, while I immediately understood the impact and the cost of the man's hurtful words, I didn't understand *why* it would even happen in the first place. I wondered, "How could he not know that he was hurting himself, as well, by doing that?" In fact, we were *all* instantly affected by the chaos created in those moments.

My mother, through her own unique spiritual perspective, later attempted to explain to me why such things can happen in this world—that most human beings just don't remember our infinite connection to one another. And most didn't have the benefit of understanding through an experience such as my own. So, that was one of those moments when it became clear to me that not everyone experienced and understood that underlying truth. I also realized that there were probably going to be many more surprises along the way as I continued to step farther into the depths of this new and interesting existence in which I now found myself to be.

CHAPTER 16

NEW MEMORIES

"I could never forget that we are all born of the same underlying Source, and therefore, infinitely connected... forever inseparable."

A S SOME MEMORIES OF my life prior to the journey slowly began to return, they often somehow felt like someone else's memories. It seemed as though I was creating new memories with a new "operating system." And I was also not concerned about any gaps regarding those old missing memories. They were of no real concern to me because everything happening in the present was so much more interesting! Besides, I assumed that I would be able to remember whatever was important as the need would arise. If not, I would most likely just respond in a natural, unattached, and spontaneous manner. Again, the past just didn't seem so important anymore; a feature that would remain throughout my life. I was not (and am not now) enamored with the past. In fact, this is probably why I have so easily lost track of things like photos, gifts, and especially any objects of my childhood that I'm sure must have had sentimental value prior to my Near-Death Experience. No matter how wonderful some of those experiences and *things* may have been, I have never longed to re-live or hold on to them.[13]

Of course, I soon realized that we all have been naturally endowed with the capacity for storing memories, some of which may be pleasantly useful and sometimes critical for helping us continue along our worldly evolutionary paths of life. And some may even appear, if only temporarily, as challenging and unpleasant obstacles along the way. However, I came to the realization that there is always the possibility of new and wondrous experiences to be had at any given moment, and whether we label them as good or bad, they are all there to continually move us forward towards the fulfillment of our life's journey.

But the most important memory? I had not forgotten what I had seen and learned through my death experience about who and what I really am, that we are all born of the same underlying Source, and therefore, infinitely connected throughout the entire creation. That could never be forgotten... ever.

I Have a Wife?

There was yet another significant detail that had escaped my memory, along with all the other memories that had initially vanished following my return to the body. I was quite surprised when I was informed that I had a wife! I was told of this news very soon after I had left the hospital and had gone to recover at my parents' home. She apparently had come to visit me at the hospital shortly after the surgery. Of course, I had no memory of that, but I was naturally eager to meet her (again?) as soon as possible and hoped that she might also open the door to the return of even more memories. Arrangements were made for us to meet at my parents' home and while this was a somewhat awkward situation, particularly for my family and my wife, I was excited about this new chapter in my continuing journey.

There was a palpable sense of relief for everyone as soon as I saw her face and looked into her eyes. I did remember her and began to have more memories return as we continued to talk. There was a pattern emerging that would prove to be key for triggering more of the lost memories. I would often start to remember people, places, and events that had been occluded from memory as my wife, family, friends, and acquaintances shared stories of their previous time with me. But not always. (*Back then and to this day, there are many "pre-NDE" memories that remain inaccessible, no matter how many times and by whom the stories are shared.*)

Back to the City

A few weeks after meeting with my wife, I decided that I wanted to move back to Dallas to be with her as soon as I was physically able. So, just as I had convinced the doctors at the hospital to allow me to leave earlier than they would have liked or recommended, I convinced my father to take me back to Dallas earlier than he thought was advisable. In fact, looking back now, I'm surprised he went along with this idea. I was still very weak and hardly had the stamina to walk very far at all. And I certainly was not equipped with the kind of important memories that would be essential for living in a big city. But I was stubbornly persistent in my determination to return to Dallas and so my father relented, and thus began yet another new chapter in my second act!

Upon arriving and having my father help me out of his truck and carry me into the apartment, I felt my wife's sense of apprehension as she realized just how physically fragile I was and how challenging it might be for her to balance managing her work schedule and care for me, as well. But I promised it would be alright and that I would not put too many demands on her. Even so, I knew it was going to be difficult for her.

CHAPTER 17

OLD FRIENDS FALL AWAY

*"I had changed so much, quite literally
overnight, that they felt they had lost the person
who they knew me to be before my death
experience. Our paths had diverged."*

S HORTLY AFTER RETURNING TO Dallas, we had the
opportunity to move to Denton, Texas and reunite
with many of our old friends with whom we had worked
back at the time of that tragic nightclub event in Fort
Worth. They were all very happy to see that I had
survived my health crisis and welcomed me back with
open arms. Of course, they weren't prepared for some of
the major changes that had taken place in my life and
soon became aware that I really wasn't quite the same
as before. I was still "me" but after having gone through
such a life-changing experience, our mutual interests were
obviously even more different than before. I continued to
enjoy my meditation practice and began to attend a few
meditation retreats while creating new friendships with
more like-minded individuals in that regard.

Even with my rapidly expanding interests and new friends and directions, I still accepted all my old friends just as they were. We had been like family for so long and I loved them all dearly. I never felt compelled to force my truth on anyone else because I knew that we were all in the midst of our own individual journeys and were free to travel whatever paths that resonated most for each of us. But, once again, they were finding it increasingly difficult to relate to me and my new path that appeared so different than before. So over time, one by one, those old friendships began to fall away. And finally, even my wife decided to move on in her life without me. She had initially made the effort to try to understand and adapt to the new "me." She even learned the meditation method that I had learned, but it was not her natural inclination to do so and, in the end, like most of my old friends, she ultimately fell away, too.

I understood and accepted why all of this happened as it did. I had changed so much, quite literally overnight, that they felt they had lost the person who they knew me to be before the "journey." So, again, over a relatively short period of time, they had all gradually moved on. I did not fault them in any way and only wished them all the highest good, as I also continued moving forward with my life. And while I had never shared with them, or anyone else, the story of the amazing life-changing events that took place during my time in that hospital room, I could already see that it would present its own unique challenges along the way. I accepted that reality as part of the "price of admission." It would never be possible to deny what I had witnessed in those precious moments of my journey and now it would continue to serve as a foundation for all the uncommon events that were about to unfold in my life.

Body Not Ready for Prime Time!

After about nine months of having to depend so much on others to help in my recovery process, I felt it was time to see about becoming more self-sufficient. Even though I certainly was not back to 100% physical strength, I decided to look for some work that I could handle to get myself moving again. I landed a simple job working in a nearby discount department store and was excited to be starting my first day. Everything seemed to begin well enough, but the job did require me to be on my feet most of the time. After the first couple of hours, I was thankful when the break time arrived. I sat down and chatted with some of the other workers until the break was over. When I tried to stand up again, I couldn't bend my knees! They were frozen into a 45 degree-angle and there was nothing I could do to get them to straighten again. I had to call someone to come to pick me up (literally!) and take me home. My body had apparently not yet fully recovered from the joint and muscular atrophy caused by the sustained essential mineral depletion and extended period of physical inaction during my long stay in the hospital. This premature effort to work resulted in another 3 months of recovery time. So much for self-sufficiency!

After this setback, I committed to be much more proactive in giving my body the essential nutrients it needed and I added incremental strength conditioning exercises, as well. Once I was able to add bicycling into my regimen,

I knew there would be no more physical setbacks. I was finally able, once again, to experience the physical joy of being in this body after all its struggles over the past two years or more. And now, I believed I was ready to add yet another significant activity that would not only exponentially accelerate that joy, but that would spontaneously open a door to even more sublime experiences that had begun during the journey.

CHAPTER 18

MUSICAL BLESSINGS

"I had literally and completely transcended the activity of playing the guitar, as I slowly began to notice that there was an audience coming into view."

B ACK WHEN I FIRST left the hospital to begin recovery at my parent's home, I recalled that someone tried to explain to me that I was a professional musician and that I played drums. I was somewhat surprised to hear that because I had no memory of that, like so many other missing memories. I wondered, "Where are my drums?" And then, "Will I even remember how to play?" I had no idea how to make that work. Since this was so early in my "re-entry" phase, I didn't have enough experience yet with how this "memory thing" worked. So, I wasn't sure if I would actually be able to play the drums again. However, at that early time I was barely physically strong enough to walk more than a few feet without becoming exhausted, so it was not something to give much consideration to right then. I would not have had the physical strength to attempt to play drums, even if I were to suddenly remember how to do it. I was sure that sometime later, I would get around to trying it out.

For now, though, there were many other outstanding issues at hand to deal with, including learning how to become a vegetarian, as required by my doctors. In fact, I could only eat pureed cooked vegetables for quite some time until my digestive tract was fully back online. Even then, there would be no consumption of any meat for an indefinite period of time. Thankfully, my sister had already become adept at being a vegetarian and over time, she helped me become quite accomplished at it, as well. In the meantime, there was a lingering fascination with the idea of playing drums.

A little over a year or so, after going through all the various stages of recovery and regaining my strength, especially after the temporary setback following the latter attempt at trying to work, I felt it was time to get back to that idea about playing drums. Now that I had the physical strength, I was at least ready to give it a shot. Plus, I had recently been listening to lots of music and had the opportunity to watch some local drummers perform with their bands. I was getting the feel for it and eventually located my drums and began to play. Much to my surprise, I could play reasonably well right away. Of course, I was a bit rusty but the inherent memory of how to play was still there. After all, I had begun playing when I was only nine years old and played professionally right up until my health crisis in 1972. So, it seemed reasonable to expect that I might be able to pick it up again close to where I had left off before. I also soon realized that my ability to effortlessly learn new music and new technique seemed to come at an accelerated rate. (This was a phenomenon that I much later discovered was a direct benefit of how my brainwave function had somehow been altered as a result of going through the death process and the subsequent journey.)

The Joy of Drumming 2.0

I was able to pick up a gig at a local club that had a lighted, computerized dance floor and a live DJ spinning records of all the popular music at that time. My job was to be set up on the stage with the DJ and play drums to whatever he put on the turntable. This gave it a live band feel and it gave me an opportunity to play many different styles of music, which I very much enjoyed. It had the extra benefit of helping me to develop perfect timing. You can't get off beat in that situation. The records don't lie when it comes to tempo and timing!

Eventually, I began to play with other musicians in the area and that's when the magic really started. Playing was such an effortless joy for me and there were many times while playing on stage that I literally transcended the activity of playing. I didn't stop playing but my awareness was in an almost unbounded space, similar to the experiences I had in meditation, and similar to some of the experiences I had during the NDE. There was absolutely no effort or strain in those moments, and I felt a deep connection to the other players, as well as to everyone in the audience.

Witnessing My Performance

I recall one such experience while performing on stage with four other musicians. We were having a great time playing together and there was a very natural connection amongst all of us—in the pocket! During one song, which was a more dynamic, up-tempo song, I began to perceive myself and all the other players from just above the stage. I could look down and see us all, including myself. This was not an "Oh my gosh!" moment. On the contrary, it felt as natural as before it happened but with an added subtle depth of peace and stillness. Even during the dynamic physical activity being executed in the performance, there was still the simultaneous subtle witnessing of what some might consider a seemingly uncommon experience.

As the experience continued, I noticed a faint, soft translucent blue thread coming from the heart of each of the players, all of which connected to my heart.[14] It was as if we were all connected and playing from one source in a perfect and sublime space. I was simultaneously witnessing the creative impulses contributed by each player, all coming together like points of data that fluidly ebbed and flowed back and forth amongst all of us. Of course, the audience had to be affected by this, as well, even though they had no idea what I was experiencing at the time. In fact, there was a thunderous applause when the song ended, which brought a close to the more expanded, almost boundless experience that was occurring during the performance. Now, we would bask in the rousing applause from our audience for our exciting performance!

Transcendence While Performing: Perfect Stillness

Over the years, I often experienced more subtle gaps of a deep stillness while playing my drums and at times when I performed on guitar. Another such experience occurred after I had moved to Fairfield, Iowa where I was participating in some advanced meditation programs. I was asked to play some of my more subtle instrumental guitar compositions for a meditation course graduation ceremony. As I sat before the audience, playing one of my songs, there was a point where I had literally and completely transcended the activity of playing the guitar. The only way I knew that had happened was when I slowly began to notice that there was an audience coming into view and only then did I realize that I was playing my guitar in front of a room full of people! I momentarily had the thought as I continued playing, "Well, I hope I wasn't just sitting there doing nothing. That would be awkward!" But my fingers were still moving, and I knew that I had continued playing even as I had transcended the whole process. I finished the song and took a nice long deep breath. There was just a profound silence in the room, and it seemed like an eternity before there was any applause. But once it finally started, it was quite a show of appreciation that went on for a while.

After the program had ended, a few people came up to me and shared what they had experienced during that performance. Many of them had also transcended along with me during the song. That's when I more clearly understood why it took a little while before the applause began. There was a stillness in the room that was palpable and there really wasn't a need for applause at that point, as far as I was concerned. I could have just sat there for a while longer and continued to enjoy the peaceful silence. I appreciated their quiet presence and subtle awareness that helped make it possible for us all to have such an unbounded and sublime experience.[15]

These kinds of experiences continued at various times throughout the years of my music career and still do now and then to this day. Playing drums and guitar has always provided a nourishing and stabilizing means for integrating and maintaining that deeper experience of connectedness to the subtle fabric of the creation—just as I first experienced it all those years ago through the journey that truly was and continues to be "the gift that keeps on giving."

CHAPTER 19

DESCRIBING THE INDESCRIBABLE

"How does one describe something that is quite nearly beyond description?"

T HE JOURNEY ALWAYS REMAINED fresh in my mind, but I still had not told anyone what had happened or the details of what my experiences were like now. At first, I didn't have the words to clearly express what had unfolded as I went through the death process and the subsequent return to my body. How does one describe something that is quite nearly beyond description? How does one speak of things that seem outside the realm of what is generally accepted by others to be "normal" life experiences? Especially if it falls outside the lines of the more traditional, conservative beliefs and teachings regarding life, death, and "the beyond." Furthermore, it did not occur to me that there was any pressing need to speak about it for quite some time. That is, until one fateful day when there seemed to be no other choice but to share it for the first time....

Excitement!

It happened five years after the journey while I was attending a large meditation retreat. The primary purpose of the retreat was to participate in large group meditations, but there were also numerous lectures available on a wide range of topics related to the development of consciousness. I decided to go to one of these lectures, but I was running a few minutes late so when I entered the lecture hall, I quietly sat down next to a friend in a back row seat. I had just missed the introduction, so I was initially a bit confused, as it was not what I had expected. That's when I realized that I had gone to the wrong lecture hall!

In fact, it turned out to be a lecture on Quantum Physics, of which I really knew nothing about, or so I thought at the time. I considered getting up and trying to make it to the other lecture hall, but I didn't want to seem disrespectful to the professor who was obviously very excited about his subject matter. So, I sat quietly and tried to pay attention and perhaps learn something about a topic I had vaguely heard mentioned before.

After a while, I started to get more and more interested. Not only that, but I was also starting to feel a growing sense of exhilaration as the professor started describing a theoretical quantum particle that somehow seemed very familiar to me. Then I suddenly jumped up out of my seat and declared, "That's right!" You could have heard a pin drop at that instant as everyone turned around and momentarily stared at me. I quickly sat back down with eyes facing the floor and waited for the lecture to end so that I could make a fast get-away. When that moment arrived, I blasted out and went straight to my room and closed the door behind me, hoping no one would find me! But as fate would have it, someone almost immediately knocked on my door.

Now What Was That All About?

It was my friend whom I was sitting next to at the lecture. Although I was not prepared for it, I knew what she was about to ask. "Now, what was that all about?" After a few moments I replied, "Are you sure you really want to know?" She immediately exclaimed, "Of course I do!" So, I said, "Well, alright. Sit down because I'm going to tell you something that I have never told anyone, and I don't have any idea how long it will take or even if I can find the words to clearly express what I'm about to share with you."

But first things first. She wanted to know what the reason for that crazy moment was when I had jumped up out of my seat at the lecture. I explained that the professor was describing a theoretical particle as the first and subtlest particle that could lead to more and more subsequent particles in a unified field of creation. I got very excited about that because at the farthest and most refined point of my journey, I very clearly perceived a precise particle that fit that description perfectly. In my experience, I saw it as the first or last particle, depending on which direction consciousness was moving at that point.

Then there was the rest of the story to share with my friend. I just began, not knowing if I could truly express it in a way that would at the very least not be confusing but ideally could enliven within her a sense of that infinite connection we all share with the underlying essence of the creation. At first, I wasn't sure if I could find the words to most accurately describe the subtlest details of the experience. But the words seemed to come forth effortlessly once I started. I was, after all, able to perfectly describe the entire journey from beginning to end. It took between two and three hours, but in the end, it felt completed.

It was actually a great relief to finally share for the first time the most intimate and powerful experience of my entire life. And when I finished telling the story, it felt as if a great burden that I had carried with me for so long had now been lifted. Of course, the journey itself was anything but a burden. I would go through it again and again if I had to for what it revealed to me and how it had impacted my life, and undoubtedly would continue to do so. But not knowing how or if I would ever share it with anyone else had always quietly weighed on my mind after walking alone on the path it was laying before me. And I only just then realized that there was a simple gift of healing for others that could come through the telling of my story.

CHAPTER 20

WHY I SHARE MY STORY

"... but if my story brought a value of healing to others, then I knew that it was always meant to be shared."

THERE WERE MANY INTERESTING experiences that occurred for both of us as I shared the story with my friend. I had initially assumed that she might have many questions once I started but instead, she sat quietly and just listened intently throughout most of the story. I appreciated that, as my intention was not to "teach" anything but rather to simply share the story and allow her to come away with whatever value that she may ultimately draw from hearing it. I knew that was my only role in the process.

There was a deepening sense of connection between us as I looked into her eyes while speaking. I often felt as if I were looking into my own eyes and could see how the story was creating a softening, natural unifying coherence all around us. Sometimes I would just pause in moments of silence and then continue on. There was absolutely no strain or effort throughout this time for either of us.

I did pause at one point when I noticed that she had some tears welling up in her eyes. I asked what her tears were about, and she said she didn't really know why it was happening. She just felt a wave of emotion rising up that was not attached to anything specifically that she could identify. It was apparently just some emotional release that spontaneously came to the surface. After a few more moments of silence, she encouraged me to continue.

The Divine Presence

At some point along the way, I began to notice a very subtle shift in the room. At first, there wasn't really anything visual but there was a specific space in the room where there just seemed to be a slight fluctuation or very subtle movement in the air. I was faintly aware of it as I continued, but it was not a distraction or cause for shifting my attention away from carrying on with the story... until it was. What happened next was an amazing and powerfully uplifting experience for both of us.

The fluctuation I had initially become aware of was changing and becoming even more visually perceptible. Now, it could certainly not be ignored. It was not frightening in any way at all, but it had our full attention. I began to see a growing collection of very subtle particles of shimmering light and something faintly beginning to appear within the particles. As the particles subtly increased in density, it became clear that the "something" that was faintly appearing moments before was actually a "someone" that was manifesting before us. Then there was not just a visual perception but also an undeniably powerful but deeply peaceful and comforting quality that filled the entire room. We then realized who this being was and could see his face cradled amidst all the shimmering particles. It was the presence of Jesus.

He did not speak to us but exuded an incredible essence of love that was truly beyond what words could ever express. And we were immersed in a wave of deep peace and stillness. Then, within moments of this recognition, the manifestation began to fade. For what seemed like several minutes, we just sat there, speechless but with an incredible sense of peace and gratitude.[16]

Healing of Old Fears

A few days later after sharing the story, I asked my friend how she was doing since our recent experience. She said that she felt so much lighter and that some old lingering fears from past experiences that she had been carrying around in her life for years seemed to have faded away. I assumed that could probably be attributed to the special manifestation that we experienced when I was sharing the story with her. That would have been the most logical explanation at that point in time. But she thought it might also have been influenced by hearing the story of my journey. Either way, I was happy for her and was not attached to the how or why of it. I was just glad to know that something was lifted for her and that she was experiencing a new level of ease and peace.

It was inevitable, however, that she might share her experience with others and that is exactly what happened. I was soon being asked by others if I could share my story with them. I must say that at first, I was slightly reluctant to step into that arena. It was, after all, a new experience to have shared for the first time with my friend and I wasn't sure how others might react or if they might place certain expectations on me that I would not be comfortable with. I was still in an evolving process of integrating my experiences into this life and finding a balance between "the two sides of the coin," even though it had been five years since it all started. Nevertheless, I agreed to share my story with a few others when they asked.

It didn't take very long at all before I realized that the experiences and understanding I gained through my journey were not for my benefit alone. I could see a pattern of healing taking place for those with whom I shared my story. Many people were (*and are—that's why there are countless books of the subject*) initially fascinated by the phenomenon of the Near-Death Experience (NDE) and were curious to hear if I saw departed loved ones, saw Heaven, angels, or even Hell, and any number of other "flashy" experiences. But after hearing my story they always came away with something more than what they had expected to hear or experience. Most importantly, they consistently reported the same results after hearing the story: some release of fear that they had been struggling with, sometimes for nearly a lifetime.

There have been times when I ran into someone with whom I had shared the story a while back, and I'd ask how they've been since then. I often heard the same thing. Some old fears seemed to have fallen away, very quickly and spontaneously. I recall one particular response that stood out to me when I asked how a person was doing and he said, "When you told me your story, it changed my life!" I was surprised by his response and asked what he meant by that. He said, "I'm just happier. I don't sweat the small stuff like I used to." Of course, I was only sharing the story and there was no discussion about resolving fear or solving other problems. It was as simple as the first time I shared the story with no agenda other than to simply tell the story. How it affected those who heard it was not actually my concern. And I don't know why it has always had this effect, but I don't question it. Again, these kinds of responses helped me to understand that my journey was not just for my own personal benefit, but if it brought a value of healing to others, then I understood that it was always meant to be shared.

CHAPTER 21

OCCLUDED LIFE REVIEW

"It was absolutely the most intense experience I had ever known in my life or could ever imagine!"

S O, LIFE CARRIED ON and over time I was more at ease and always happy to share my story when asked. However, there was the fact that I lived in a world that, on the surface, requires a level of collective agreements and expectations. We mutually participate in certain structured norms, traditions, beliefs, and so forth. One of those norms is that we ideally engage in productive activities that result in the accumulation of money and the accompanying "stuff" it acquires. Therefore, over the years, I learned various skills to sustain myself in this world. But the one activity I really excelled at and enjoyed the most was playing music and particularly playing drums. It had an integral role in helping me reintegrate after my journey. It was grounding and expansive at the same time. And of course, much as I felt when I was 12 years old and got paid at the end of my first professional gig, it was still an amazing feeling to know that I could have so much fun playing music as an adult and still get paid for doing it! I've spent much of my life playing music for a living, even as I've added other supplemental skills, as is sometimes required for musicians during the times we call, "in between gigs." But playing and touring was always my primary occupation.

I would often be out touring for weeks at a time, return home for a short period, and then head back out again. When having to be away for long stretches of time, it was always special when I had the down time to relax, visit with family and friends, and enjoy other activities. During one such break I invited a close friend over just to hang out for a while. We decided to watch a movie (*VHS back then!*). It was titled "Jacob's Ladder." I didn't know much about it other than I heard it had received critical acclaim and was generally considered to be a very complex but interesting movie. It turned out to be a very psychologically disturbing movie. As it was ending, it triggered a feeling that I only rarely ever had but I felt like there was something big about to happen that seemed beyond my control.

Intense!

When the movie ended, the video tape went all the way to the end and produced that snowy appearance on the screen along with the loud hissing sound. As I stood in front of the TV and pushed the off button, the normal "click" I expected to hear sounded like a loud cannon going off and I immediately went into an intense experience unlike anything I had ever experienced before, or so I thought. At that moment it was like a curtain flew open in front of me and I was thrown deep into an experience that had already happened all those years ago shortly before I was leaving my body, but that had been occluded from my memory until this particular moment. I always knew there was something about those time gaps that I couldn't remember and whenever I tried to uncover what that might be, I felt some unease and trepidation about pursuing it any further.

It was the "life review" I had obviously gone through during my death experience. It was not like remembering something that I had simply forgotten. I was living through it as if it were the first time I'd experienced it, in real time! It moved so fast that whatever the scenes were, it was impossible to discern one from another. It was an intensely overwhelming conglomeration of rapid-fire bits of flying shards that contained the data of everything that had happened in my life right up to and just before I left the body during the crisis in the hospital. It was absolutely the most intense experience I had ever known in my life or could ever imagine. What made it so incredibly intense was that I got to experience, all at once, the impact my every thought, word, and action had on not just other human beings throughout the entire planet, but how it also touched every single possible particle of the entire infinite field of creation, from the most densely manifested levels of creation that we are generally most familiar with to the subtlest, barely manifested particles. This intense experience was almost more than I could bear. And only after it ended did I instantly realize why it was initially occluded from my memory after I had made it through the death experience so long ago. I was in such a weak and fragile condition back then that I'm sure I was mercifully spared the memory of this life review. It would have been much too intense and may have been the one thing that could have prevented me from returning to and remaining in the body after the journey.

I have no idea how long I was standing there in front of the TV. I imagine it was only for a few moments, but when it was over, I just turned around and looked at my friend who was sitting on the couch. I couldn't speak at all. I was overcome with emotion, and I literally felt drained. I made it back to the couch and sat down. My friend just instinctively put his arms around me and held me as I began to weep. He knew my story, so he felt that this obviously had something to do with that and he was just there for me, without any judgment. He knew there was nothing for him to say or do other than to just be there as my friend. That was all that was needed and all anyone could have done.

I could do nothing but cry for nearly an hour or longer before attempting to explain to my friend what had just happened. There really wasn't that much to explain. I knew I was now entering a process of deeper healing and evolution, even though I had no idea how that would continue to unfold or what the final results would be when it was completed. I trusted that I would come through it in time. How much time was yet unknown.

After a while, I began to settle down a bit and told my friend that I knew what this was, and that I would be alright. I'm sure he was not certain of that, but I gave him my assurance that I would call if anything came up that I needed help with. I just asked that he not say anything to anyone about this and that he would not try to have anyone intervene. I knew the last thing I needed now was for any mental health professionals to come in and interfere with this process. It would be almost impossible for them to understand, and they would most likely try to label my experience as some kind of psychotic breakdown. My friend agreed and left with the understanding that he should just check in on me periodically. Oh yes, and make sure I had whatever food and supplies I might need. There was no way I was going to leave the house until I got through this new process that I understood was a necessary part of my continuing journey.

Enhanced Perception

In the subsequent days, I was in a hyper-sensitive state, both physically and emotionally. I could not watch any television and even with my love of music, I had to be careful what kinds of music I listened to. There were days when all I could do was curl up on the floor and just cry, sometimes over the simplest things like song lyrics that I had always enjoyed but now found to suddenly trigger some sense of sorrow and loss. Everything was significantly intensified, so I had to keep it simple and avoid being overloaded with sensory input. Even when something did happen and I felt overwhelmed by it, I still knew deep inside, as if witnessing the moments from afar, that this would pass and there would be some new level of experience or awakening.

This process continued for about one month and then suddenly, as quickly as it had started, it just ended. Something had shifted and there was a sense of great clarity and rejuvenation. What I didn't realize at first was that there was also a shift in my perception. I became more aware of this after I left the house and reengaged in socializing with friends and acquaintances. There seemed to be an enhanced quality of silence in the background of activity. My sense of auditory perception was more refined.

There were instances when I was sitting in a busy restaurant or a place of commerce where people were engaged in quiet conversations. Occasionally, amid the noisy cacophony of multiple conversations and other sounds, I would spontaneously begin to hear individuals talking at a table that was far away from where I was sitting. They were far enough away that their voices would have been completely beyond the range of regular auditory perception. It was as if someone had turned down the volume of everything else and amplified the specific conversation. Sometimes this could be almost comical and other times more serious. In fact, in most cases, I would have preferred this not happen at all.

I also noticed that some electronic equipment would stop functioning when I touched it, especially whenever I was excited. I learned to monitor myself to make sure I was settled before handling certain kinds of devices, especially computers. I couldn't wear digital watches, as they stopped working almost immediately when I put them on. So, I had to wear the old simple non-digital styles of watches.[17]

More Gifts to Come

There were other subtle changes happening which I didn't realize at that time were preparing me for a more significant development of expanded perception. These changes in perception would be essential for the spontaneous emergence of some healing gifts I had no idea were going to come within the next three to four years. In the meantime, I just carried on with my life and began to be more comfortable and accepting when these kinds of new developments started to manifest from time to time.

CHAPTER 22

MOTHER'S PASSING GIFT OF LIGHT

"I felt a sensation of being wrapped in a warm blanket of golden light, as I became aware of the sublime presence of my mother..."

O N A COLD IOWA winter morning, I received the call that no one ever wants to hear. My mother had suddenly collapsed and was rushed to a hospital in Dallas. The initial diagnosis was systemic stage 4 cancer. Both the family and doctors were astounded, as no one had any idea that Mother had been seriously ill and that she could have gone so long without complaining of any pain or discomfort. This disease had obviously taken some time to reach such a critical stage. Of course, we all knew that she never really complained much about anything. She was always the first to comfort us whenever we were struggling, whether it was regarding physical or emotional issues. Mother was first and foremost interested in caring for the happiness and well-being of her family. Right or wrong, she just didn't want to burden us with her own personal challenges that she felt could possibly cause us worry or concern.

A Race Against Time

As I was in the process of making travel arrangements to Dallas, my sister called and said it was urgent that I get there as fast as possible. Mother's condition was rapidly deteriorating, and it appeared that she would not recover. She had been moved into a private room and all my brothers and sisters, along with my father, were already at Mother's bedside. I was the only one missing and I desperately wanted to be there to be able to speak with her while she was still conscious and tell her how much I loved and appreciated her. I was certain that she knew that. Ours was such a powerful bond but I wanted to be there with her and my family in those precious moments of her final transition.

I was able to book a flight out of Iowa and would arrive in Dallas that afternoon. But on my way to the airport, I received a message that due to a severe winter storm my flight was rescheduled for the next morning. I could only hope that Mother would hold on for just a little longer.

After a restless night, I was finally on my way. By the time I arrived, Mother had already slipped into unconsciousness and was no longer speaking. I had missed that opportunity to hear her voice one last time. But as I stood next to her bed and took her hand in mine, I knew she was aware that I was finally there to be with her and our family. I also knew that, even though she appeared to be unconscious, she could hear our words. She could feel our love for her. Of this I was certain, having gone through my own death experience all those many years ago.

Indecision

Even before my arrival, there had been an ongoing discussion amongst my family about what Mother's wishes were regarding her medical directive. She and my father had discussed this quite some time ago so that they would be prepared for how to handle such a situation as we were now faced with. Her doctor had said that he could possibly do some procedures and treatments that could prolong her life for just a little longer, but it would be grim at best. However, there was nothing further he could do to save her life. The doctor understood how difficult these situations can be and was graciously awaiting a decision from the family if we wanted him to go forward with any other treatments.

So Mother was "on hold" for a while longer as the family had these difficult conversations. There was some conflict about whether to just accept her and my father's wishes, or whether to prolong the inevitable. Daddy, my sisters, and I were on the same page. We wanted to honor Mother's wishes and let her pass peacefully with hospice's assistance. However, my two brothers were holding onto the possibility of a "miracle." They felt that God works in mysterious ways and maybe we should allow for that possibility.[18] This holding pattern became somewhat frustrating at times, especially for my sister, Barbara. She was adamant that we should simply honor

Mother's wishes. We all knew that it was ultimately my father's decision to make. But I think he also wanted to respect my brothers' feelings and therefore, allow them to work through their process. I knew that at that point in time, they just weren't ready to let Mother go.

We were at an impasse and a decision needed to be made. So, I privately approached the doctor and explained the situation. He had been my parents' family doctor for many years, so I knew it was difficult for him, as well. But I asked him to put that aside and just tell me straight up the hard facts of this case. Once he did that, I returned to share his assessment with my family. At that point, my brothers were able to agree, and we were finally on the same page. I knew that Mother was ready to move on, but she always wanted harmony in the family, so I felt that was what she was waiting for.

We returned to Mother's room and quietly gathered around her. There was a rich silence that permeated the room as the machines that showed her vitals were very softly beeping in the background. Then the hospice representative entered the room and gave my father some release papers to sign. We really didn't know how long it might take Mother to make her transition, but we were told it would not be long. Immediately after my father signed the papers, he stepped away to go to the restroom and would quickly return. However, an amazing thing happened immediately after he gave his signature and left the room. Mother's vitals had been slowly but steadily dropping lower and lower. We knew this was her time to pass. But my father had not returned yet. "Someone go get Daddy!"

Release

My sister, Barbara, was standing at the head of the bed and gently resting her hands on Mother's chest to be certain when Mother took her final breath. She did this so she would be able to tell our father when Mother finally passed because we were not certain that he would make it back in time. While he was away, we continued taking turns softly talking to her and telling her how much we loved her. I knew those words, "We love you, Mother," were the most powerful and meaningful words that she could ever hear in those moments. It was not only our way of showing her our appreciation for what her life meant to us, but it was also our way of releasing her and letting her know that it was now ok to leave this world behind. She could go on and continue her journey, unencumbered by any need to worry about us. Her work here was complete. She could leave knowing that she was truly loved. However, I knew Mother was really in charge and there was no way she'd leave until Daddy was by her side.

By this time, we had all fallen silent as we wondered if each shallow breath might be her last. Then my father walked in and immediately stood next to her bedside, took her hand and said, "Oh, she's gone!" But my sister said, "No Daddy, she's still here. She waited for you." He was so overcome that he couldn't speak. I could see the pain in his eyes but what was even more powerful was the extraordinary love pouring from his heart. Mother was the love of his life from the first moment he had met her and throughout over 50 years of marriage.

So now Mother's earthly journey was over as she took her last breath. While each one of us experienced her passing in our own unique ways, we were all blessed and united by Mother's incredibly powerful love. She left us with special gifts of love that we would carry with us throughout the rest of our lives. One of those gifts was immediately received by my sister, Barbara, as our mother's soul left her body.

Right after she had told my father that Mother had waited for him to return, Barbara felt the moment Mother's soul left her body as it passed through the top of her head and right into and through my sister's heart. The rush of this experience was not only very powerful, but also intensely joyful. So much so that she could hardly contain herself. She said that it lasted for a very long time, and she felt Mother wanted to give that experience to her. In fact, she says that she can still feel it to this very day whenever she chooses. This was Mother's "superpower." The gift of unconditional love.

Mother's Healing Presence

The hospital had been our world for a few days so after Mother's passing, Barbara, Daddy, and I went to his home to rest and then prepare for others in our extended family to join us. As soon as we walked through the front door, only then did we realize how exhausted we were. We each went into separate rooms to lie down and rest before others arrived. As I lay on the bed, I hardly had any energy left to even begin to process everything I had just experienced. I didn't fall asleep, but I began to settle into a quieter state of mind and body.

After a while, something unusual began to happen. I started feeling a sensation of being wrapped in a warm blanket of golden light. It was even more than a sensation. I literally began to visually perceive a faint, almost translucent gold light slowly moving up over my body. This was the same golden light I had experienced many years ago during my own death experience. It gave me a very deep sense of peace, as I felt the sublime presence of my mother. I knew it was her way of comforting me, as she always did throughout my life.

After the golden light had faded, I immediately got up and walked out into the hallway to go find my father and sister to tell them about what had just happened. They were already standing in the hallway and said they had also just experienced Mother's presence. While to some this might have seemed to be quite an unusual phenomenon, we felt it was just like something Mother would do. Again, it was her way of comforting us and showing her appreciation for having been there with her during her time of transition.

Only a short time later did I realize that her visitation was the catalyst to a whole new path that was about to emerge in my life. Additionally, there were to be other times when I would occasionally experience her presence. I knew she was there in certain circumstances to gently encourage me to honor the gifts of the "journey" and to be strong in fulfilling that purpose as it continued to unfold.

CHAPTER 23

GOLDEN LIGHT REVISITED

*"A fine mist of brilliant gold particles of light
filtered down through the treetops, filling the
air all around."*

OVER THE YEARS, I periodically had experiences of a presence of the golden light; the same light I had experienced during my journey and once again on the day of my mother's passing. One early evening, as I sat alone in the woods enjoying the stars above, I looked up through the trees as the color of the sky began to change. A fine mist of brilliant gold particles of light filtered down through the treetops, filling the air all around. Everything it touched, the branches, the leaves, the air itself, became infused with the golden light and as it moved closer and closer towards me, it finally entered my chest and quickly filled my entire body. As I looked down at my arm, which now appeared translucent, I realized that this was the same golden light I had experienced all those many years before.

I have no idea how long this experience lasted but after a while, I left the woods and headed back home. As I drove into town, I became aware that the value of time had dramatically changed. I looked into the rear-view mirror at one point in time and saw an intersection that I had obviously just driven through. I wondered if I had stopped at the stop sign, but I had no memory of it. I had slipped back into the only time where everything really happens—the present, moment by moment. Nevertheless, I found my way back home and decided that I should just go to bed and stay there, as it was probably the safest thing for everyone! Although I'm sure that I must have stopped at that intersection... at least I think I did.

Timelessness

For the next few days, I didn't sleep, and I don't recall ever eating during this time. I lay down to sleep, but there was no difference between sleeping and being awake. I also never lost any sense of awareness and never for even a moment felt tired or disturbed by the experience. It all seemed to flow with a steady evenness and an underlying continuum of deep peace and silence. There were long periods of time when I was sitting up in bed and was aware of the faint presence of a being sitting directly in front of me. I could never see any details of a face or body but there was a soft, glowing white luminescent quality that filled the immediate space before me. I had a sense that something was silently being communicated to me, although I never heard any words spoken and for some reason it did not occur to me to speak, either.

This altered state of time, or timelessness, continued for five days, after which I had to get back into activity and drive to another city for a scheduled interview, rehearsal, and a week of musical performances. These various activities would, of course, require the presence of mind and focus to effectively accomplish them all. It could prove to be an interesting experience, to say the least.

Grounding Human Touch

I stopped in at a local restaurant to pick up some bottled water before leaving town. As I walked in, I saw a friend who was sitting with a small group of people. She took my hand in hers as she said, "Oh, Thomas, I want to introduce you to my friends." I instantly felt a sense of grounding the moment she touched my hand and was quickly pulled back into what could be considered a normal state of time. Then again, what is normal? After this helpful encounter, I settled into a state of mind that seemed most appropriate for managing the various details of the job that lay before me.

CHAPTER 24

EMERGENCE OF THE HEALING GIFT

"I began to be able to see into subtle aspects of physiology and spontaneously enliven and accelerate a person's natural healing processes."

E VERYTHING WENT SMOOTHLY IN the following days during my travels. As I was driving home, I began to feel some subtle tingling sensations and warmth in my hands. It was as if my car's steering wheel was hot to the touch, although I was aware that the actual source of the heat was emanating from my hands and not the steering wheel. I wasn't sure what was happening in that regard, but I was not overly concerned about it.

I went to visit my girlfriend at the time after returning from my short tour and saw that she was using crutches to walk. She had sustained a severe ankle injury and her doctor said that there was some damage to her tendon. She was scheduled to return for a follow-up appointment to determine what further treatment might be required. In the meantime, he advised her to rest and keep her foot elevated as much as possible. When we sat down on the couch, she put her foot up on a pillow next to where I was sitting. I don't know why, but I had an impulse to hold my hand over her foot as we were conversing. Much to my surprise, I suddenly began to see inside her ankle. This was not anything I had expected and had never experienced before, yet it somehow seemed very natural and certainly not shocking in any way.

I felt heat coming from within her ankle and could see a pervasive red color throughout. Then I saw something that looked like an old rusty, crusty spring. Of course, I knew it wasn't a spring, but I didn't really know what it was. I soon began to see a violet color appear and then the object just suddenly began to dissolve and fade away, like water over sand. The initial red hue had gradually changed to a soft white blue. She experienced a cooling sensation and then got up and walked across the room and back without a limp or any pain. That was it. She never had a problem with it again.

This is when I discovered that I had spontaneously acquired some ability to help facilitate healing. I could only assume that this was a gift that was bestowed upon me during those few days following the experience of the golden light in the woods. I began to be able to see into subtle aspects of physiology and simply through innocent observation, without any judgment or intention to manipulate, I was able to spontaneously enliven and accelerate a person's natural healing processes. In addition to the release of physical pain, illness, and emotional trauma, individuals experienced a deep, peaceful silence along with an expanded state of awareness. This expanded awareness also enhanced their ability to experience the silence of that same unbounded Source that I had experienced during my NDE several years before.

I had already been speaking to more groups and organizations on the topic of Near-Death Experience prior to the emergence of this healing gift, so I naturally began to include these healing sessions during and after my presentations. As a guest speaker at an International Association for Near Death Studies (IANDS) event in Chicago, I offered to give a group session to the 300 guests in attendance. There were many profound experiences, which I attributed to the enhanced collective consciousness of such a large group. Afterwards, many individuals wanted to schedule personal sessions. In fact, there were so many session requests, I had to extend my stay in Chicago and soon acquired office space in Evanston where individuals could come for personal sessions.

Can You Teach Us?

People began asking, "Can you teach us how to do this?" I really had no idea how I could do that. There was no school to teach it. No one taught me. It was just a gift. I had never set out to learn any of this. At first, I didn't even understand how it really worked so how could I teach it? All I knew was that it worked. But they kept asking, so I finally said, "If I ever figure it out, I'll call you and let you know."

Then one day as I was riding my bike along the Lake Michigan trails in Chicago, not thinking about this or anything else for that matter, just riding and enjoying, suddenly it flashed right before me! In an instant I knew everything I needed to know about how to teach this. It was as if someone had just handed me a complete manual with every detail of exactly what to do. I immediately turned around, raced home as fast as I could, sat down, and started typing the "manual" as fast as my fingers could move. It was all there. One of my close friends said, "It's a download! You got a download!" Whatever he wanted to call it and however unusual it seemed to have happened, I knew without a doubt that this "download" would certainly work. I called those most persistent clients and asked, "Are you ready?" They said, "Yes!" And so, they came. My first weekend training program went flawlessly, almost like magic. It was fulfilling to know that I was no longer alone in this work, that others could do this, as well.

Since that first training program, I have continued to teach people how to use this Healing Spectrums Method for the treatment of others and as a self-treatment method, as well. Medical doctors, psychologists, physical therapists, chiropractors, and mental health care professionals are having wonderful results using the Healing Spectrums Method as an alternative adjunct treatment in their practices. But others, from all walks of life, are learning to use this simple method as a complementary adjunct for bringing greater health and wholeness to themselves and their families and friends.

I have continued this work for over two decades and have been blessed to have witnessed some amazing transformations, physically, emotionally, and spiritually, for countless individuals during that time. After thousands of individual and group sessions over the years, I have been inspired by the amazing ability of the human body and mind to grow and evolve into higher states of coherent functioning, all for realizing our greatest potential and purpose for being.

A New Mission

While I am grateful for all the events that have led me to this life's work, I know that we are all very special and have many gifts to share with one another, even if some may not yet know what their unique gifts are. Learning to trust our intuition and embracing the art of non-resistance to what simply is in any given moment can naturally cultivate living in the present. That is where joy lives. Not in the past or in the future. It is in those moments where our inherent gifts gradually begin to surface. This is just how it naturally unfolded for me, as well.

In time, I have come to understand why everything in my life happened exactly the way it did. Every day I am thankful for the blessings of these experiences, even the ones that I sometimes may have initially judged as negative, only to realize later how I benefited from having had such experiences. Each experience can bring with it an opportunity for growth and evolution.

My mission is simply to share with others the gifts and revelations of my journey that can potentially help them live healthier lives with greater joy and inner peace, knowing that infinite, eternal Source within. This is my life's work, and the journey has only just begun.

PART 3: A DEEPER LOOK BEHIND THE SCENES

CHAPTER 25

NDE OR FINAL TRANSITION?

*"Whether through a Near-Death Experience or
that final transition of life,
there is no right or wrong of how we should
experience either journey."*

T HE REASON FOR WRITING this book has always been to share the story of my journey and the revelations of the wholeness of life that is possible for all human beings. Some may think these experiences are unusual, super-natural, or perhaps possible for only a few who have had a Near-Death Experience. But I view it as the birthright of every human being to come to know and live our fullest and most sublime range of being. We are all infinitely connected to the underlying essence that gives rise to and sustains the entire field of creation. That essence from which we can never be separate.

Of course, I could never claim to know the evolutionary path of anyone's soul, nor how one will experience either a

Near-Death Experience or one's ultimate passing from this worldly existence. My hope is that anything I share here in this book will simply inspire others to consider and seek out a path of unlimited possibility.

A Continuum of Life

I have always believed that sharing one's Near-Death Experience is not just for the benefit of the experiencer, but they are for the benefit of others, as well. Each NDE is unique and perfect for each individual. While there are often certain similar experiences such as a tunnel, a brilliant light, greetings by past loved ones, angels, and more, there is not one "right" NDE or even a "right" final transition, for that matter. At the very least, sharing these experiences may potentially help ease the fear of death. But more importantly, it may simply remind us of the eternal nature of life; that we are much more than just human beings contained within the boundaries of a physical body. Life truly is eternal.

I have had the opportunity to share my own NDE many times over the years and have always found it to bring comfort and hope. I have also been blessed with the opportunity to be present throughout this transition process with others and their loved ones. I say "blessed" because it is truly a blessing to witness and be a part of such amazing moments. I have witnessed birth and I have witnessed death, and in all sincerity, I can say that there is a particular moment in that transition where there is only life.

Whether it be birth or so called "death," that special moment is one and the same and only leads to a continuum of life.

Of course, it is never easy to lose a loved one. It is difficult to watch as their body is engaged in a losing battle to continue to exist. But through witnessing my own death process and that of others, I can assure you that there comes a time when it simply becomes a physical process, and the essence or soul of the person is not suffering while the body appears to struggle in its fight for survival. The body is programmed to survive and will do all it can to function until it can no longer continue on. But other things are happening behind the scenes. The individual consciousness ultimately transcends the physical, beyond the reach of pain and suffering, as it is silently preparing for its transition from its worldly form.

There are many special gifts that are bestowed to others during one's transition. Sometimes we can experience these gifts as they unfold or perhaps sometimes later as we move through our grief process in our own way and in our own time. There is no set formula. There is no right or wrong of how we should experience that loss and ultimate healing, just like there is no right or wrong way for anyone to go through the NDE or that ultimate transition.

For those of us who have had a Near-Death Experience, there is an undeniable sense of the eternal nature of life.[19] Even though we may no longer exist in the form that we came to know and identify ourselves as being in this physical world, we know that we never cease to exist. For others, sometimes it is just a matter of faith that we do continue. We just each do the best we can with it all and appreciate the opportunity to have shared in life.

But there is also an inherent possibility of experiencing something very powerful and positive. When we lose a loved one, there is often an amazing outpouring of love and support that can reassure us that in the end, it's all worth having had the opportunity to live, love, and be loved in this world.

CHAPTER 26

LIFE CHALLENGES AFTER NEAR-DEATH EXPERIENCE

"What the individual really needs is just to be accepted and to feel supported as they work through the struggles they face reintegrating after going through such a life-altering experience. Their reality has changed."

OVER THE YEARS, I have often had the opportunity to meet others who have had a Near-Death Experience. In some of those cases the white light would appear and, as in my own experience, most were naturally drawn towards it, without any hesitation. However, in other cases, the light would appear, but the individual did not immediately choose to move towards it. Something else was temporarily drawing his or her attention at that moment. Although there was not an immediate movement towards the light, it remained in the background until finally, the attention was drawn back to it and the individual then began to move in the direction of the light once again.

In a few rare instances, some individuals saw the light but could not move towards it. They were pulled in another direction, a direction that sometimes was not necessarily pleasant! Perhaps there was some lingering attachment to an old fearful belief so strong and overpowering that they simply could not let go and allow themselves to naturally move on. The following is one such example:

Some time ago, I received a phone call from a church pastor who had heard of my story and wanted to talk to me about his recent NDE. It was, indeed, quite a different experience than mine. This gentleman was one of those "hellfire and brimstone" pastors who always preached to his congregation about a terrible place where the souls of sinners could end up for all eternity. He was deeply attached to this idea and so it was not at all surprising that when he was dying, he never even saw the light but instead, was immediately drawn into the space he feared the most. Even though he was "a man of the cloth," he still believed he was unworthy and could not possibly go anywhere else upon his demise.

It was a terrifying experience that shook him to the core and left him in such a disturbing state of mind that he found it exceedingly difficult to continue in his ministerial role. I felt sorry that he had to go through such a horrible experience so I shared something with him I hoped could possibly help him understand how or why he might have been led to have such an experience. I explained how just as we are responsible for creating our own reality in this worldly existence, we can sometimes carry some of that with us across that momentary threshold of death. One could think of it very much like the backdraft of a speeding vehicle. The air seems to be sucked in right behind it. So, if there is an overly strong attachment for the need to continue to have a particular belief or intention when we leave the physical body, then we could possibly and very likely bring that along with us in the beginning of our journey. It can be either liberating or, as in the pastor's case, terrifyingly oppressive and nightmarish.

Then there were others who were so frightened by the sudden realization that they had left their bodies, panicked and fought to quickly return to the body. Many of these individuals had become so attached to the dense physical reality of the world we live in that they were overtaken by the fear of losing it. If they lost that, what would become of them? Would they simply cease to exist? And of course, as mentioned above regarding an overpowering fearful belief, some were afraid of what unpleasant consequences may await them. Here is one such example:

I spoke with a retired police officer who had previously been shot in a gunfight. He told me of how shocked and frightened he was as he saw his mortally wounded body lying on the ground as he fought to get back into it. Anyone would naturally have that kind of initial reaction. That was not unusual. But he went on to say that he was terrified of what would happen if he died. His whole identity was all about his work, and his immediate friends and family, his activities, his car, his home, etc. He never really entertained the idea that there was anything more. So, when he thought he was dying, he was suddenly fearful that he would simply disappear and not exist in any form whatsoever. That would just be the end of him and that suddenly was not ok! This experience was so troubling that he had to retire after physically recovering. Since he had never had any kind of "spiritual experience" that could have given him any sense that there might be more, he had tragically lived with that fear of death every day thereafter.

Finally, there are many who did not see any light at all and simply returned with only the experience and realization that they seemed to exist even beyond their mortal bodies. Just this extraordinary knowledge, alone, is enough to change a person's life forever. It presents an entirely new way of experiencing and understanding the vast creation we live within. It can soften the contrasting edges of reality and bring an expanded sense of our own true nature.

My own experience with the light was very simple and straightforward. There was no hesitation, distraction, or distress that altered my direct path into the light and beyond. So, after hearing many of these different experiences from a wide range of individuals from various walks of life, I understood why it was so easy for some to move towards the light, while it was more complicated for others.

I have often been asked, "Why wouldn't everyone have the same experience, assuming that there might be some basic, universal truth or constant reality after we leave these mortal bodies?" When considering such questions, I have become accustomed to reflecting back on the totality of my own Near-Death Experience. In doing so, I simply fall back on some of the most fundamental experiences of the journey, all of which ultimately lead back to that most powerful moment of creation: The Birth of Consciousness. It was in that instant I understood that consciousness is the catalyst for creation, that *I* am consciousness, and therefore, I am a willful participant in the creation of my reality. Of course, we are all doing just that all the time, no matter where we seem to exist in any level of creation, whether we know it or not.

Again, I have often said there is not one right Near-Death Experience. No one experience is better than any other. Each one is perfect and right, as it is based on the evolutionary state of consciousness of the individual at any given moment in time. So, when I have also been asked what one should do, how one should experience their own journey through the death process and beyond, my answer is always this: If at all possible, and probably not the easiest thing to do for obvious reasons, just forget about everything you ever thought you knew. Your soul knows exactly what to do. Trust in that and, as the saying goes, "Let go and let God."

Reintegration

I had shared in an earlier chapter in Part 2 some of the challenges of reintegrating after my death experience. The biggest challenges I faced at first were primarily physical in nature. I didn't really struggle at all regarding what I had experienced in my journey. I didn't have the contrast of any previous memories influencing my thoughts or emotions because I didn't initially have a past when I returned to this life, at least for quite some time. However, once I rejoined being with my wife and my old friends, there was the obvious situation of how they were all challenged by the significant changes in me.

Over the years, I've had the opportunity to speak with many individuals who had varying degrees of NDEs. I realized that my reintegration was different than most because I initially had no expectations. I was simply operating from the knowledge and experience of my journey and wasn't attached to any past that had existed prior to my NDE. I wasn't attached to much of anything as much as I was enjoying the new discoveries of my new life as it was unfolding. But as I mentioned before, that didn't work so well for those who had expected that I would return the same as I was before. It was more about others' challenges of how to relate to me. Even if I had initially thought to share my journey with them, I really don't believe it would have changed that dynamic. In the end, it was just easier for them to gradually distance themselves from me for their own comfort level. Ironically, I wasn't troubled or saddened by this. I cared about them, but I understood that I would never be that person again that they wanted me to be. And that was ok with me.

For many others who have gone through an NDE, it is often very difficult re-integrating because they generally remember everything about their lives that came before, and they can feel the pressure of others' expectations. Family and friends often think there is something wrong with them because they find the person's behavior to be very strange. What the individual really needs is just to be accepted and to feel supported as they work through the struggles they face reintegrating after going through such a life-altering experience that they themselves don't even quite fully understand. It can take time to settle back into society and still be authentic to one's own way of being without giving into the temptation to pretend to follow others' ideas of who and how one should be. Once a person tries too hard to *fit in*, at the expense of their own authenticity, then they can feel even more isolated and misunderstood. It takes patience and compassion from both sides.[20]

Fortunately, there is a great organization that does understand and that can help these individuals get through the difficult initial stages of "re-entry." The International Association for Near Death Studies (IANDS)[21] has been studying this phenomenon for decades and offers special presentations, workshops, and other helpful events. In fact, it is a very positive, safe environment for helping those who have gone through a NDE in their new journey of reintegration, as well as helping family and loved ones gain a better understanding of the NDE and how to be more supportive of their loved one.

CHAPTER 27

THE GRACE OF DEATH

*"Finally, there is a special moment when all
suffering stops and one is able to clearly
experience freedom from pain and fear, yet still
be present within the body. It always happens."*

I N MANY OF MY talks and radio interviews, I have often
discussed some of my experiences in helping souls in
transition. While my work is mostly devoted to helping the
living evolve and grow into greater health and wholeness, I
have had my share of experiences regarding the transition
of souls. Sometimes I work with individuals to help
them prepare for and to go through their own imminent
transition. Although it certainly can be a difficult thing
for some to accept at first, there comes a time when one
can begin to more gracefully accept and embrace the
experience. Just as birth is an amazing and intense process,
death is equally amazing and intense.

While we observe a loved one who is in the final stages
of the death process, they often appear to be suffering.

Perhaps we are troubled by the difficulty and shallowness of their breathing. Their brow may be furrowed, and they seem to be struggling to cling to life as their body fights to survive. It is important to remember that the body is programmed to continue the fight until the very last breath. This can be emotionally overwhelming for family members who are present and witnessing this stage of the process. Of course, it is understandable because we don't want to see our loved ones suffer. However, what we are viewing is a natural process of the physical body attempting to function for as long as possible until it is no longer possible to do so. If we could see what is really going on in the background, we would realize that the consciousness or the soul of the person we are viewing is busy elsewhere and not always involved in that physical battle for survival. This is especially true once the later phases of the process have begun. The soul has other things to prepare for while the body fights its own battle.

There is one very important point that should be noted at this stage of one's transition. Quite often we may have the natural and spontaneous impulse to soothe or console our loved one by gently stroking either their hand, arm, or even their face. There is certainly nothing wrong with that intention. However, as a person is in the deeper stages of their transition and as they are approaching the final moments leading up to that transition, this action can be a potential impediment to the ease of their process. They are steadily withdrawing from their physical body and this worldly plane of existence. It is a letting go of any attachment to this world.

Speaking from my own experience of going through this process, I can say that there is a hypersensitivity to touch, and it can be, in the best case, somewhat of a distraction and in the worst case, unpleasant and even a source of agitation. It can be a subtle stimulus, even momentarily, to be drawn to the corporeal form the soul is attempting to be released from. Just simply holding a hand without moving and very softly speaking these simple words, "I love you," is all that is really needed.

Finally, there is a special moment when all suffering stops and one is able to clearly experience freedom from pain and fear, yet still be present within the body. It always happens, even if only for a fleeting moment. I know, because I have gone through all of it myself, in my own death process. I have also witnessed this occurring for others at precise moments before their ultimate transition. I suppose it could simply be a way of being left with the final memory of having had the opportunity to fully experience the evolutionary physical manifestation of being human. And again, witnessing both birth and death, there is that brief special moment in the transition, coming or going, when there is life on either side "beyond the veil of life and death."

CHAPTER 28

UNDERSTANDING THE SENSE OF LOSS

"Even when we understand the greater reality
of the eternity of being, it is most important that
we fully honor our true feelings as they arise."

W HY DO WE FEEL such a sense of loss, sorrow, and grief when a loved one passes on? It is never easy to experience such a profound loss, but this is rarely ever a question that we would ask in those emotionally difficult moments. It may be a question we might later consider (*or not*) as we move deeper into our own unique journey of healing. For those who may now be willing to delve more deeply into this question, I hope to share a perspective from my own journey that may potentially provide greater peace and understanding.

So, what could be the underlying source of this overpowering sense of loss and grief? We mostly identify ourselves and others by what we do, think, eat, wear, and drive, by our jobs, religious beliefs, philosophies, intellect, humor, our physical appearances. The list goes on and on. These are just the outward characteristics and expressions of who we are being in this world. Again, all this is not the definition of *what* we actually are. However, this seems to be the general manner of how we define and relate to one another as human beings. It may, therefore, be the primary basis for our own fear of death.

What if all those qualities are taken away, as in death? What would be left? Isn't that person then forever gone from our lives? Aren't we then truly separated? Does he or she still exist somewhere? What exactly is it that we mourn the loss of? We have heard from my own experiences, and from those of countless other individuals who have gone through the death experience, that there is much more to all of us than meets the eye. When we leave this mortal body and all of its more densely manifested qualities, we find that we continue to create, perceive and experience; albeit a much more refined level of perception and experience which is, nevertheless, still experienced through that same individual consciousness that previously occupied the now deceased body.

We cannot truly be separated by the physical boundaries, at least as I have come to experience and understand. Every aspect of creation is eternally connected by that same underlying silent Source. In fact, the physical boundaries that appear to separate us from one another and from the rest of our perceived creation are sometimes just a bridge to the illusion of separateness! Again, it is not only entirely possible to simultaneously experience the underlying unified value of wholeness along with the uniquely expressed values of the individual boundaries; it is ultimately our divine purpose and birthright as human beings.

So, the sense of loss we feel is really about the loss of all the familiar qualities and attributes of our loved ones that we have come to identify them as being. Yes, they have ceased being expressed through those qualities and attributes, but they have not ceased to be. They can never "not be" and, therefore, can never truly be separate.

If we consider this as a possibility of the reality of death and the eternal nature of the soul, we have the opportunity to more graciously move through the bereavement process in a way that can ease our level of suffering. We can more effectively be there for others, who may not have come to the same realizations about death, to help support them through their own healing process, as well. However, even when we understand the greater reality of the eternity of being, whether through a simple faith or through a direct experience, it is most important that we fully honor our true feelings as they arise. It is not helpful to resist any feelings of sorrow or to pretend that we are not deeply affected by this kind of loss. To do so would only hinder our full healing and, therefore, unnecessarily prolong any suffering we may experience in our healing process. Even a great saint mourns the loss of his or her beloved teacher.

Likewise, it is also important to move through the bereavement process and be willing to release ourselves from the pain and sorrow we have experienced during that time. It is a journey that should ultimately come to an end;

at least, in the healthiest of outcomes. It is a journey from which we can emerge with a greater appreciation for the life of our loved ones; but most importantly, one which can lead us towards a fuller understanding and experience of the eternal nature of all life.

Letting Go

I recall an experience I had during a presentation to a bereavement support group for individuals who had lost loved ones. There was a tradition to go around the room before the presentation began to allow each member to introduce themselves and state why they were there. Each briefly spoke about the circumstances of the death of their loved one and how it affected them. They also stated how long they had been members of the group. At first, I was a bit surprised by how long some of them had been in the group, in some cases, for several years. I thought about what an enormous burden it must have been to have carried the weight of such sorrow and remorse for so long, as well as the cost of the potential to move forward in their own lives.

After the introductions, I began my presentation, which included an abbreviated version of my NDE, followed by a question-and-answer segment. Throughout this time, I gradually became aware of an increasingly subtle but steady change in the room. There was a growing feeling of lightness in the air and a more vibrant appearance in the faces of the members. However, there was one couple who had lost their son to suicide. They had been struggling for many years with an overwhelming sense of guilt and remorse that they should have done more—that they should have done something more that could have prevented that tragedy from happening. (*This is not an uncommon emotional response in these kinds of deaths.*)

At this point I shared with them the one thing their departed loved one would want to tell them if they could: "I am sorry for any pain my actions have caused you. But I am ok now. Please don't let my passing stop you from going on with your lives. Even though I am no longer with you in a physical form, I will always be with you. I will always be a part of you. The greatest gift you could give to me would be to let go of your sorrow and find renewed joy in your life. You deserve to have that now and always."

By the end of my presentation and the Q&A segment, there was a palpable, vibrant liveliness that permeated the room. The overwhelming heaviness that had initially filled the room was completely gone! Everyone seemed to have been released from the tenacious grip of their sorrow long enough, hopefully, to come closer to their own emotional healing. Perhaps it was an opening to reclaim a part of themselves and their lives that had been shut down for so long. It was gratifying to see a sparkle return to their eyes that only an hour before had all but been extinguished by their grief.

It is possible that we can have both a more enlightened understanding of death and the eternity of life, along with the natural human emotions we feel when dealing with the physical death of our loved ones. After all, we are human beings living, learning, and evolving within a field of simultaneous unity and diversity; of boundaries and the unbounded, uniquely expressed values supported, sustained, and permeated by one essence. There is life and then there is life, all sustained by the underlying, unmanifest Source that gives rise to it all.

CHAPTER 29

WITNESSING THE TRANSITION OF OTHERS

"Our eyes were completely locked in with each other. No need for words. I held her hand in mine and as she gently closed her eyes, a brilliant white light completely filled the entire room."

Diane's Friend

I HAVE HAD MANY opportunities to be present during other's transitions, being asked by friends and sometimes even by individuals whom I didn't know but who had heard about my experiences and felt I could be helpful in some way. In almost every case, my presence was more for the families who were struggling with the imminent loss of a loved one. After all, the soul of the person who is transitioning knows what to do, especially once they have entered the later stages of the process. It is always a very delicate time, and I am careful about honoring the family's tender emotions. My role is to quietly connect with their loved one first and then reassure the family about the subtle process that is taking place beneath the outward appearance of their loved one that could otherwise be perceived as suffering.

I recall a very special case that happened while I was in Chicago, giving a series of presentations and personal consultations. I received a call from the director, Diane, of the local IANDS organization asking if I could come right away to be with her dear friend who was in a hospital and very close to death. I had never met Diane's friend before, but I was told that this person had heard about me some time ago and had always wanted to meet me but just had not been able to do so. Now that she was nearing the final stages of her transition, she asked if I could come to see her. I naturally agreed and arrangements were made to pick me up and drive me to the hospital. I was informed on the way that timing was of the essence, so I immediately began a Healing Spectrums session to connect with Diane's friend. After a few minutes, I told Diane that she needed to drive faster because I could feel her friend was very close to passing.

When we arrived, I was rushed to a room where a few family members were gathered. After a quick introduction, I immediately went to the bedside to connect with Diane's friend. She reached out to me and took my hand. She tried to speak but was not able to get the words out. But that didn't matter. I expressed to her how honored I was to be with her now and that everything would be alright. Our eyes and awareness were completely locked in with each other and even though there were others in the room, it was as if only the two of us were present in those precious moments. The connection we had simply transcended the need for any words. There was only an incredibly deep sense of peace and love between us.

Then, as I held her hand in mine, she gently closed her eyes. I suddenly felt a powerful exhilaration and there was only a brilliant white light that completely filled the air. There was nothing else in my awareness but that. Everything and everyone had become one with that light. In a few moments, as the brilliant light began to fade, there was a beautiful stillness in the air. I knew she had made her final transition. And what a powerful transition it was!

I gradually became aware of others in the room, but no one spoke. I finally heard the steady monitor tone that activates when one has passed. I was surprised at how long it took to be activated after I knew she had already left her body. I thought to myself, "That equipment isn't refined enough to be able to measure the moment a soul departs the body." (*In fact, sometimes a soul departs even before the final breaths.*)

A few minutes later, I went to a guest room to allow the family to be together alone with their loved one. Later, when asked, I shared with them what I experienced with her and told them what a deep sense of peace and love she experienced in those final moments. I also expressed how much I appreciated the opportunity to be there and what an honor it was to be a part of her transition. I knew there were some in the family who probably were not familiar with my story, but I was glad that they were willing to honor her wish to have me there. As always, I offered to be available to speak with them again if they would like.

Molly

Molly had miraculously survived a terrible car accident but sustained severe injuries that left her paralyzed. It was apparent that she would never be able to walk again and for someone who was very active and loved to dance, this was a tragic outcome. I remember visiting with her in the early days after her accident. Sometimes she would try to present a positive attitude but mostly she struggled with anger and depression about her situation. Her health began to fail more and more over time and there seemed to be nothing anyone could do to bring her out of her sorrow.

Then one day when I had been out riding my bicycle, I stopped to rest for a few minutes. I felt a shift in the energy all around me. There was an overwhelming sense of calmness along with a simultaneously expanding energy filling the air all around me that began to extend upwards and into the sky. Then suddenly, the sky was filled with that golden light that I recognized once again. In that very moment I felt Molly's essence everywhere.

When I returned home, I was told that Molly had passed away. It was, indeed, at the very time I was experiencing the golden light that was filled with Molly's presence.

I knew she was now free from that broken body that could no longer serve her soul's evolutionary path. She was free.

Marvin

I received a call from my cousin, Pam, that her father had suddenly and unexpectedly passed away from complications of an aneurysm. She asked if I would go with her to the hospital to see him and to help her with whatever initial arrangements needed to be made at the hospital. When we arrived and entered the room, the nursing staff had already removed any monitoring equipment and had prepared Marvin's body for our viewing. After a few minutes of silence, we both commented on how he just looked as if he were sleeping peacefully. A few moments later, I had an unexpected but not altogether unfamiliar experience.

I observed Marvin standing just to the right of his body that was lying in the bed. He had such a joyful expression and was completely at peace. Then after a few moments, he slowly faded away. I took a few more minutes before I told Pam what I had just witnessed. In other situations, it might have been something that I would have kept to myself and not mentioned, at least right away. But I knew Pam would want to know. After I told her what I had seen, she smiled and said that was just like something Marvin would do. He was a beloved long-time meditation teacher who understood and believed in the eternal nature of the soul. He, of all people, would have no fear, resistance, or regret of his soul making this peaceful transition.

In Summary

Each case is unique to each individual when their time of transition comes but there is always a common underlying thread that unites them all. There is that magnificent liberating moment when the soul is finally released from the physical body. No matter what level of physical suffering one may have endured before, it is all over and forgotten in the final moments leading into that release. While most individuals may not have the ability to perceive the most subtle aspects of their loved one's transition, it is, nevertheless, important to trust in that understanding—to trust that the soul is in charge and knows exactly what to do in this process for its own highest good. It can also help us in our own paths of healing from the emotional pain and sense of loss when a loved one leaves this worldly plane of existence. But if we believe that a soul's journey is eternal, then we can believe, therefore, that life is eternal... nobody dies.

CHAPTER 30

DIVINE BEINGS

*"The angels are simply there to help facilitate
the physical and emotional healing of the
individuals who are present."*

I HAVE BECOME AWARE of the presence of the different angels quite often during some of my presentations and group sessions. The healing angels are always present but on rare occasions, I have experienced a different "divine" presence. This happened once during a presentation I was giving to a local IANDS chapter in Chicago with an audience of around 300 individuals. I always like to treat the audience to a group Healing Spectrums session at a certain point in the presentations. The larger the group, the greater the collective consciousness seems to enliven an even greater value of coherence. That enhanced coherence is conducive to a more refined level of perception not only within my own awareness, but also for many others in the audience.

As I began the session, I briefly instructed everyone to close their eyes and sit comfortably without any attachment to any particular outcome. In this way, they could just be innocently present to whatever experience they may have without any expectations. I also had no expectations or attachments to what anyone, including myself, should experience during the session.

Once we began, I very quickly became aware of several healing angels throughout the auditorium. They were particularly drawn to be with some individuals who later shared with the group that they had been dealing with some difficult physical or emotional issues. The angels often appeared to stand in pairs immediately behind those individuals, as they always do when they are present.

As I continued the session from my position on the stage, I felt the presence of someone standing just behind me. Then I felt a hand gently resting on my right shoulder. In that instant, I realized who this divine presence was. It was the manifestation of Jesus. When this happened, there were really no words to describe that moment. It was the deepest, most sublime experience of peace and love. In that moment, I knew there was really nothing for me to do other than just trust that everything was absolutely perfect.

I don't really have any idea how long he was with me but as I brought the session to a close, I was able to fully engage with the audience and was no longer aware of his presence. There were several individuals who had also become aware of some of the angels in the room. Then there were a few who asked the question, "Was there someone up there with you? Who was that?" I had not mentioned anything about that and wasn't certain that I would, but it seemed the decision had just been made for me. So, I delicately shared who it was and what I experienced during those moments.

The reason I considered whether to share that experience with the audience was because I was not sure how they might respond. I never want anyone to think this is something that I have any control to "make" happen. Nor does it make me more special than anyone else. I have always been very clear that when sharing the gift bestowed upon me after my extensive death experience, my role is simply to innocently share it without attachment to any sense of ownership or ego, and I am very clear that it is something to always cherish and honor. I am never tempted to manage or manipulate anyone's experiences during the sessions. I would not even know how to do that.

What I Know About Angels

There are a few common questions I have often been asked during some of my talks and radio interviews over the years. But I'm always surprised when asked about angels: "Are there really angels? How can you see them? What do they actually do?"

Being brought up in the Catholic faith, I certainly saw my fair share of angels. However, they were always presented in the form of statues, in the stained-glass designs throughout the church, and images in the more elaborately designed bibles. I, too, often wondered if they really existed. After all, prior to my NDE, I had not seen a real, living angel, so like other extraordinary phenomena of this nature, I could only consider the "possibility" that they were real but could never be certain. In fact, to this very day, my approach to such questions is that if I have not actually had a direct experience with such phenomena, then I just consider it a possibility, but I cannot confirm or deny its reality. Furthermore, even when I do have such an experience, I am not inclined to pursue a more extensive study of it. I just accept it as my own reality, based on my own direct experience. I can simply share it with others and leave it up to them to delve into more thorough studies if they feel so inclined. So, I was not initially certain of the existence of angels... until I was.

It happened one day, many years ago, as I was driving through downtown Fairfield, Iowa. I suddenly noticed a very large angel standing by a tall building spire and looking out over the city. I suppose it could have been one of those moments of, "Wow Look at that! That is amazing!" But that was not my reaction at all. Instead, I felt a deep sense of peace and security. It somehow just seemed perfectly natural in those few moments. Only later did I consider that at long last, I could confirm that angels were real, at least to me.

I began to witness their presence more often, especially during my talks, sessions, and training classes. Aside from that very tall angel that was approximately 25-30 feet tall, which I rarely ever saw after its first appearance, I noticed that there were different kinds of angels. Some were small, some more the size of humans, and some much taller that were 8-10 feet tall. They all seemed to have different roles to play as they appeared under certain circumstances. Thus far, after many years, they almost never acknowledge my presence except on the very rarest of occasions. Even then, I have never heard them speak and I have no idea if they have names, but I am aware of why they are there and what they do. They are simply there to help promote the physical and emotional healing of the individuals who are present. While there may be others that I am not aware of and that may have different purposes, I have observed four different kinds of angels thus far:

The Protector Angels

These are like the first one I ever saw that was standing by the downtown building spire. It appeared to be quite powerful and on guard for the protection of the city.

The Watcher Angels

These angels are typically 8-10 feet tall. They usually stand in a corner, away from the people sitting in the room. I call them Watcher Angels because they seem to silently observe what is happening in the room. They will occasionally and suddenly appear right next to and just behind an individual. This usually happens if a person is in a deep state of distress or is releasing a very old and significant emotional trauma. Their movement from the corner of the room to the individual is not a gradual movement. It is instantaneous. Less than a split second! At that point in time, I have no idea of how these angels are ministering to the individual, but I know the person is "in good hands."

The Healing Angels

I have observed that there are always two Healing Angels present for every person. One appears to be for physical healing and the other is for emotional healing. Both are closer to the size of humans. They place their hands on the individual's shoulders and somehow aid in the release of some physical and/or emotional release.

Again, I have no idea how they are facilitating the healing process but the person they are with quickly begins to settle into a more relaxed state and there is a noticeable release of the tension in their face and body.

The Transition Angel

This is probably the most powerful angel I have ever experienced. It is extremely rare to see. I have only witnessed its presence at the moment of one's final transition, what we call "death." I later discovered that it can sometimes appear after a loved one has passed but a family member seems unable to move beyond a deep state of grief for some time. However, its most common appearance is at the time of transition and is manifested in the brilliant white light that completely fills everything in that moment. Sometimes this angel is barely perceptible in the overpowering flash of the white light. When I have seen it, I can barely look at it because it is so incredibly brilliant, almost blinding to view.

I recall the first time I was able to view the Transition Angel's full form for only just a few seconds. It was during a personal session with someone whose mother had recently passed away about a month or two before the session. Her mother was the powerful matriarch of her family. Her daughter, my client, had to assume the role of her mother and take on part of managing a large family business. She wasn't prepared for such a role and had significant doubts about being able to successfully take on that responsibility. This also made it even more difficult for her to fully process and mourn the loss of her mother.

As we proceeded with the session, there was a moment of silence when suddenly, the angel appeared just above us. It was so intensely brilliant, surrounded by an even more brilliant white light. The light seemed to wrap around the sides of the angel, giving the appearance of what one might initially think of as wings.[22] After this experience, I later thought about why angels have often been depicted with wings. I can imagine that sometimes when people throughout humankind's existence have experienced the presence of angels, they may have perceived the brilliant light surrounding the angels as wings. However, as I mentioned before, these are the only angels I have experienced. There certainly could be others, and most likely there are others. It is entirely possible that some could have wings. If so, then I'm quite sure there would be a practical reason for that. Whatever the circumstances may be when they do appear, it is their purpose to aid in the healing of human beings. They help us to be free of some of the residual trauma and pain that often stand in the way on the path to our spiritual evolution and fulfillment. They are truly a very special blessing to have in our lives.

CHAPTER 31

ENTITIES, PAST LIVES, MESSAGES, ANGELS, AND MORE

"The healing angels are perfectly created for the purpose they serve and certainly don't need my suggestions as to how they should do what they do."

A FTER MANY YEARS OF sharing the Healing Spectrums sessions with individuals and groups throughout the world, there have been many notable experiences that fall into a few different categories. I share a few of these here in this chapter.

Angels

As I mentioned earlier, I have often witnessed the appearance of angels, especially during group sessions and training sessions. They don't communicate with me but generally only appear for the individuals in sessions.

However, now and then I've been asked by a few individuals who have some refined sense of perception, "Who was standing with you during the group session?" I am rarely aware of such instances because I am fully focused and present to the individuals before me, but I have observed that there seem to be two angels that aid in each person's unique healing processes.

It is important to note that I do not have any ability to direct them in their work, nor would I ever attempt to do so. The healing angels are perfectly created for the purpose they serve and certainly don't need my suggestions as to how they should do what they do. My role is to innocently allow the "gift" to spontaneously provide the value of coherence that makes it all possible to unfold in a most natural way for the highest good of all present.

Healing Grief

During a group Healing Spectrums presentation in Chicago, I became aware of the presence of a Watcher Angel standing in a far corner of the room. I just call it that because it generally stands and watches over the room. At least that is how I always observed it... until now.

There was a woman in the room who I sensed was having some uneasiness as she sat in the group. I didn't know anything about her but once I began the Healing Spectrums session, I began to experience one of those "gamma brainwave" moments (see Chapter 33/34) while my awareness was with this individual. A series of sequential images, much like a short movie clip, came into view. There was a beautiful pastoral view of a small country cottage surrounded by grassy rolling fields and hills. There was a soft summer breeze and a train track far back in the distance. It was a wonderful image of a place where anyone would certainly enjoy spending time.

At the end of that first session round, I told her what I had viewed and asked if any of that made sense to her. I knew it had to have something to do with some kind of distress for her, even though it was such a pleasant image. She said that was exactly where she had lived 10 years ago. She went on to say that it was the most wonderful and peaceful time of her life. She became tearful as she said that something had happened that caused her to suddenly have to leave her home. It was a situation beyond her control. She felt a great sorrow for having to leave it behind after which came a series of very difficult events. She had been carrying that grief with her ever since she left that wonderful home and peaceful environment. She had longed to have that again in her life.

Just as she reached an overwhelmingly emotional moment in her story where she could not carry on, I witnessed something I had never seen before. The Watcher Angel suddenly appeared right behind her with two of the other healing angels. It was not a gradual movement from the corner of the room it had been standing in. It was an instantaneous transition from one point to the other. It seemed to minister to her in some way and assist the other healing angels in their process. There was an obvious softening of her emotions and demeanor. She let out a deep audible sigh and began to have a lightness in her face that only moments before was simply a dark cloud of sadness.

We spoke later after the event, and she expressed how she felt a heavy weight had been lifted from her heart. She felt it could be possible to move on and start to appreciate some things in her life she had not been able to for quite some time, as she had been so overwhelmed by her grief. The angels seemed to have dissipated the long-standing sorrow that had overshadowed the possibility of her experiencing joy in her life.

My Guardian Angel - My Protector

We've all heard about everyone having a "Guardian Angel." I was told this early on when I was just a child, long before my later experiences with angels. It gave me a sense of comfort knowing I had an angel watching over me. Looking back at some of the crazy and dangerous things we did as children, we probably needed all the help we could get just to survive! However, even back then, I always wondered about the reality of such things that I had never seen. No one I knew had ever seen any kind of angel, either. So, it was one of those things I just had to have faith in what others had told me and hope it was actually true.

Jumping back in time to ten years after my death experience: I was working on a big construction project in Texas. We had begun to set up the large plywood forms for pouring a concrete wall on an upper level of a building. These forms were held together with many heavy clamps. There was a trench about 10 feet below around the lower foundation. This trench was an additional 6 feet deep and 3 feet wide, just enough room to bend down in to gain access for feeding some tubing and wiring through the lower foundation wall. I was tasked with handling that work and waited until the above forms were already in place so that it would be safe to proceed with my work.

At one point I was bent forward with my head down to have a better view of the opening for the tubing to go through. Suddenly someone grabbed me by the shoulders and quickly pulled me out of the trench just as one of the forms from above had come loose and fell right where I had been. If I had not been pulled from the trench at that precise moment, I would have been decapitated! I looked around to see who had pulled me out and there was no one there. No one else saw anyone there, either. But they wondered how I had propelled myself out the trench so fast. I explained that I didn't. I had no idea the form was falling and the next thing I knew I was pulled out and saved.

So even though I did not see any Guardian Angel, I was certain that one was there to protect me and save me from a horrible death. I guess Guardian Angels are real, after all!

My Healing Partner

As I mentioned earlier, I am generally not aware of angels standing with me. There have been some occasions when others picked up on some faint perception of them following along with me, especially during larger group sessions or training sessions. There was an event when this happened with a group of about 30 people present. I was giving a talk, which included my usual group session. However, I decided that instead of sitting in the front of the room to treat everyone to the Healing Spectrums session, I would walk through the room and stop in front of each person as they were seated. During this session, I held my hand up in front of each person for just a few moments until I noticed some level of enlivenment within their physiology. Once I perceived the appearance of a violet spectrum in the chest near the heart, then I moved on to the next person. After making my way through the room, I returned to my chair in the front of the room and then had everyone take a nice long deep breath and slowly open their eyes. I then asked if anyone would like to share any experiences or ask any questions.

I saw a few hands go up, but one person was quite animated and insistent on getting my attention. This was my cousin who had a specific question for me. But first she said, "I never have any experiences of any refined perception regarding angels or other celestial beings, but I was surprised by what I saw during the session." She then asked, "Who or what was walking with you as you moved through the room?" She said she was clearly aware of someone walking just behind me throughout the session. Again, I was just doing what I always do and was not aware of anyone walking along with me. I was just simply focused on being fully present for each individual. I explained that there are always angels present in the groups and that I don't really concern myself with what they do. I trust that they are intently focused on whatever their role is in those moments, and they don't communicate with me.

Also, since I'm cognizant of the fact that everyone has at least one or two angels with them when we are doing the sessions, and probably at other times, I'm sure I have one or two with me, as well.

She also wondered why she was able to experience this kind of perception when she was never able to before. I explained that we all have the ability to experience that kind of perception. It's just that we don't generally do the kinds of things that can intentionally cultivate it. But when a group of individuals comes together with a simple intention to let go and settle into a deeper state of stillness, the law of collective consciousness gets activated and makes it possible for more refined experiences.

The inherent desire of all human beings is to experience the finest value of being, closest to the Source of our existence and that of all the creation. That deep-seated intention resides within every human being. When the value of coherence is increased, such as during the Healing Spectrums sessions, that collective intention is naturally and spontaneously activated. Thus, she benefited from that enhanced coherence, which allowed her own consciousness to access a refined level of perception in those moments. It's not magic. It is just human beings experiencing more of the birthright endowed upon us.

The Imposter Angel

I never knew there could be such a thing as an "imposter angel" until I got to experience it firsthand. I was having a personal session with a gentleman who had been struggling greatly with chronic back and neck pain. We had a series of sessions dealing with this and other emotional issues. I recall many unusual experiences with him during those sessions.

Almost immediately after starting the first session, it became obvious to me that the healing angels had their work cut out for them! I had mentioned before that I generally observe two healing angels present for every human being. However, in this case, seven angels appeared. There were three on one side and another three on the opposite side where I was standing. Then there was one standing at the head of the individual. So, I sensed there was a lot going on for this person since there were so many angels present. There was apparently some "heavy lifting" for them to do in this case.

There was also something even more unusual that caught my attention. I gradually became aware of another angel standing at the feet of this person. This was odd, as I have never seen them stand at the feet of anyone in a session. So, my attention was spontaneously drawn to view a bit more detail of this particular angel and then I actually could see a face. However, I have never seen the face of an angel before. I suppose if it were important, then it would happen. But this one had the strangest, almost comical face. It was much like something one might see on a circus clown. I knew instantly that this was not an angel, but it was some kind of entity that was pretending to be an angel. It immediately vanished the moment it knew I could see it. It was busted!

I had been aware for some time that there are such things as "entities." I had occasionally seen them but never paid much attention to them. They avoid me because they cannot function in a coherent environment. The Healing Spectrums Method creates a high degree of coherence that repels them. They generally need an environment of chaos to be present and functional. They were never human, but they want to be able to have human experiences. This imposter angel tried to sneak in just as I was beginning the session. It became obvious to me how it was possible that such an entity could attempt to be present with this individual as we continued with more sessions over the next few weeks. As it turned out, he seemed to be under the influence of other more malevolent entities than the imposter angel...

Entities

I have occasionally been asked about the existence of entities. Why are they here and what do they do? Some even ask how we might protect ourselves from them. First, let me say that I do not claim to be an expert on this topic. I have seen them before, so yes, I can at least say they do exist in our world. However, I don't know why they exist, other than to create more chaos where there is already an existing environment of chaos.

As far as how to protect oneself from any entities, I would say that it is much rarer than some may think that individuals would find themselves under the influence of an entity. I always recommend that we not give them much thought at all. The less attention we have on such things, the better and the less likely we would be bothered by them. I have not seen them very often and when I do, it is usually because one has somehow fallen under the entity's influence especially while dealing with some underlying spiritual or psychic weakness, along with entertaining the general idea of entities, as well. I have also found that even when someone insists that they may have an entity causing them their troubles, it is almost never the case. It can happen, but rarely. Again, it is best not to entertain the idea of that being the cause of any mental, emotional, or even spiritual distress.

Monkey On His Back

Having said that, I can share an experience I had with the person I mentioned earlier when the imposter angel appeared. Several entities were revealed and released over the course of several sessions. One was quite interesting. Shortly after starting one of the sessions, I saw a small, strange looking entity that looked much like a monkey on the person's back. It seemed to have a grip on him and was aggressively shaking him. I could understand why he had been feeling so agitated for some time. He could not see it and had no idea it was even there.

Since the higher level of coherence had increased enough to reveal the entity, it suddenly stopped and looked directly at me. The coherence had made it increasingly uncomfortable and when it realized I could see it, it panicked and immediately ran away. There was nothing for me to do or say. I did not engage with it. These entities think we can't see them but when they realize one does see them, they become confused and frightened and quickly disappear. At least that has always been my experience.

Shortly after the series of sessions and the release of a few other entities, the mental and physical agitation he had been dealing with significantly diminished and he began to re-engage in his regular work, which he had not been able to do for some time.

Past Life Experiences

I have occasionally heard the comment, "Surely this issue I'm dealing with must have something to do with a past life, right?" My answer to that is generally, "Well, it's possible but based on many years of experience doing this work, I have found that most physical and emotional distress is created during this lifetime. There is enough to deal with in this life without having to worry about any possible past life experiences."

However, on rare occasions, there have been some sessions with individuals who were struggling with physical or emotional issues that were tied to some past life experience. In these cases, it was always associated with a very intense experience, quite often regarding how a person died in a past life. It is through these experiences that I discovered why the last thought we have at the time of death is so important.

The Angry Roman General

A woman who had been dealing with some anger issues came to see me for a session. She didn't really know why she was angry, but it was a habitual state of mind that just started happening one day for no apparent reason. There was nothing for me to do, other than to start the session the way I always do with the intention that it be for the highest good of the mind, body, heart, and soul of the individual. Thereafter, my role was to simply witness whatever unfolded through the enhanced coherence that spontaneously occurred during the session.

There was a point during a very deep state of stillness when some unusual images of the person I was having the session with began to appear. However, in this case she was a powerful Roman general who was in the middle of a ferocious battle. As the images unfolded, there was quite a bit of information about this general as he fought on the battlefield. He was a great warrior who had been in many battles and had never lost. In fact, there was an air of invincibility about him, and he believed he could not be killed. But suddenly, it happened.

An opposing soldier somehow caught him off guard and attacked him with a large sword. The thrust of the sword entered the right side of his neck and followed diagonally downward through his chest and into the sternum. It was obviously a mortal wound and he died almost immediately. But there was something revealed in that last moment just as he died that ultimately had an impact long after his death that somehow carried over and began to manifest in this woman's life. In the last moments as he was dying, he was shocked that he could be killed and then his last thought or emotion was anger—anger that he was defeated and was now losing his life.

After the session finally ended, I shared with her what I had viewed. She was quiet for a minute or two and then finally spoke. She said that every time when her anger erupted, she felt a pain that shot down from the right side of her neck and angled directly into her sternum. She had not mentioned this before the session, but it was obvious to me that what was revealed during the session was indeed a past life event that had carried over into this lifetime. She reported back later that her experiences of anger, along with the accompanying physical pain had subsided shortly after the session.

This session and others involving past life events that revealed the last thoughts at the time of death have helped me to understand the potential future impact those last thoughts can have. It is especially important to understand that letting go of anger in those moments is the best way to minimize the possibility of past life issues manifesting in a future life. In fact, understanding and experiencing the eternal nature of life now can pave the way for a more peaceful transition in those final moments, even under sudden or tragic circumstances.

Past Life Trauma

I began a series of sessions with a person who had started having intense serial dreams of dying repeatedly at the hands of her oppressors during times of war and often related to religious persecution. This was happening night after night and was quite distressing. She wondered if there was any way to end the dreams, but she also had a sense that there must be a purpose or a possible message that could be important for her to understand. Either way, she needed it to stop because it was negatively impacting her ability to focus on her work and her life.

I don't recall any series of sessions that brought about so many past life revelations. This was not something I had expected, although it seemed likely that there would be some of these experiences along the way. In fact, this often happened two to three times in each of her sessions. The circumstances in the dreams were different each time. Sometimes she was female and other times she was male, but the results were always the same. She/he was captured after nearly escaping and often tortured but ultimately killed. Each time I shared what I had viewed in the sessions, my client confirmed it was exactly as her dreams depicted.

These scenes that I had been witnessing during the sessions gradually began to diminish over time. Simultaneously, her dreams began to be less frequent, and she began to have more clarity and much less agitation. It became easier for her to engage in her work, and she soon had more energy to joyfully pursue some new and exciting projects she had put off for some time. It seemed that the debilitating influences of those devastating experiences that had so strongly manifested in her dreams, had finally been released. She could now freely move on without the weight of that past life trauma.

A Mother's Message From Beyond

There was another interesting and very rare experience that unfolded towards the end of a health-related session. During the session, there had been the spontaneous release of an artifact that revealed a very old, deeply buried emotional trauma. It appeared to be directly connected to a current digestive disorder this person was suffering from. Shortly after the appearance and dissolution of the artifact, there was an even deeper stillness permeating the room as the session continued. There began to be a growing brilliance of golden light spreading over us. At some point, the light began to pull into a more localized and focused space just above us. It was in that moment that something very unexpected happened. I became aware of the presence of someone else in the room. There was no physical form but there was a faint space that was somehow being occupied by the consciousness or soul of another being. Within moments, it became clear who this was. It was her long-ago deceased mother.

There was no audible voice or sound but just a deep, rich silence. From that silence came the message for her daughter: "I'm sorry for the things I did that were hurtful to you. I never meant to hurt you. I was suffering so much but I was doing the best I could. I hope you can forgive me." Then the light faded back to normal, and the mother was no longer present.

I shared what had just happened and what her mother's message was. There had been no mention of anything about her mother prior to starting the session. However, my client was deeply moved and went on to tell me what her past childhood experiences were like with her mother. It was a very difficult relationship and indeed, her mother had said and done many hurtful things. For much of her childhood, she could not understand why her mother treated her that way and she often wondered if her mother ever really loved her. As she grew older, she began to understand more about the emotional issues her mother had struggled with, mostly a continual state of deep depression and anxiety. She just didn't have much to give to her daughter or anyone else, for that matter.

Her daughter never had the opportunity to talk about any of this with her mother before her passing, so there never was any opportunity for resolution and forgiveness. But somehow it became possible for it to happen during the session. I asked the daughter if she now felt forgiveness in her heart. She immediately answered that she did and that she finally understood that her mother truly loved her, even during those most intense times when it was hard to see. Now she was freed from any doubt, and she felt relieved to know that her mother was also free to move on unencumbered by any unresolved sense of guilt or remorse. I felt honored to have been present for such a special moment.

A Soul's Release

During one of my tours with The Body, Mind, Spirit Expos, I was approached by someone who had heard my presentation and requested a personal session with me. She stated that she didn't really have any physical, mental, or emotional issues she was dealing with. She just wanted to experience what it was like to have a Healing Spectrums session. That was a rather unusual request, as most people are looking for relief from some level of discomfort or suffering. She was more interested in experiencing the expanded state of consciousness that is always present at certain moments during a Healing Spectrums session. In fact, this is really why I do these sessions. I've often said that if it was only about physical or emotional healing, I'm not certain that I would find that as fulfilling as helping others to experience that more expanded, unbounded state of being that we are all capable of having. Fortunately, the Healing Spectrums sessions naturally provide both.

I began our session in the same way I always do, with the intention that it be for the highest good of the mind, body, heart, and soul of the individual. She quickly settled more deeply into the session, and I noticed her breath rate sharply decreased. It was almost undetectable. This was a clear indication that the Delta brainwave was predominantly functioning in those moments even though she did not appear to be in a sleep state. I didn't notice any significant artifacts appear, other than the very faint surface stresses that tend to accumulate simply caused by the daily wear and tear of human activity.

Then suddenly, I became aware of the clear presence of another soul that was closely connected to her. It was the soul of an infant and it had been attached to her for some time. I asked if she had lost a child, perhaps during childbirth. This is when the emotional floodgates that had obviously been held in check for many years suddenly opened. She said that many years ago, she had an unfortunate situation where she had to make the difficult decision to have an abortion. She had felt a great sadness and had mourned the loss at that time, but she quietly carried with her a sense of guilt at not being able to bring that soul into this world. It was something she had kept to herself for many years.

I then understood why it was present in the session. It wanted her to let go of any further sense of mourning or guilt she may have carried with her for all that time. That had somehow held the young soul from moving on and it was time to set it free. In one magnificent moment, I was able to witness its release along with the final release of the remnant of trauma this woman had carried for so long.

A Soul's Worldly Debut

I was asked by a dear friend if I could be present for the birth of her first child. It was a home birth, and my role was simply to sit in a chair just outside the room where my friend and the midwife team were. I sat quietly and began to meditate, not really knowing what I might experience. Even though I was not in the room where the birthing was taking place, I knew it would most likely be a profound experience just being there when a new life was about to make its worldly debut. After a few minutes, I began to feel a subtle connection with my friend through a deep space of inner silence. I was only aware of her presence and the others who were there assisting her. I didn't feel any other soul or consciousness connected to my friend, at least not initially.

But suddenly, just before we heard the first sound of the newborn's emergence, I was overwhelmed by the presence of a very powerful soul about to make its grand entrance. I had a sense that this soul was here for a very special purpose, even though I had no idea what that purpose might be. It was an amazing experience to be a part of such a magnificent event. I was quite honored to have had the opportunity to be present and to help welcome this special soul into our world.

PART 4: THE HEALING GIFT

CHAPTER 32

INTRODUCING THE HEALING SPECTRUMS

*"Certain brainwave frequencies that are
known to enliven the body's healing are more
quickly activated and expressed during the
sessions."*

What is the Healing Spectrums Method?

THE HEALING SPECTRUMS METHOD is an alternative
non-touch method that spontaneously activates and
accelerates your body's natural physical and emotional
healing processes. It does not involve any diagnosis,
external manipulation, or use of any exotic devices.
Scientific brainwave studies have shown a significant
increase in brainwave coherence during the Healing
Spectrums Sessions along with specific brainwaves linked
to deep healing and regeneration, as well as an increased
state of emotional well-being.

During a session, an individual can be lying down or sitting comfortably with eyes closed. There is nothing one has to think or do, and if one happens to be trained in any specific healing methods, meditation, or other such practices, this is not the time to use them. In fact, this is the time to just "be." Simply be present to whatever is in the moment without any worry of what should, could, or might be. There is no need to try to keep the mind quiet. In fact, it is possible that there may be more thoughts in the beginning; but as the session progresses, the mind will usually settle into a very quiet state after a few moments.

The most important thing to remember before the session is to simply let go, relax, and be present to whatever experiences may come. There are no "right" experiences, as there are no predetermined or rigid expectations as to what one should or should not experience. The physiology and consciousness will lead the way and respond in the most appropriate manner.

How Does it Work?

Every human body has the inherent healing processes already built into the physiology. It is the repair and maintenance program designed to sustain and prolong the life of the body. It is a "standard manufacturer's" feature that came with the model. However, sometimes the body has a backlog of stresses or trauma that are not able to be processed efficiently. Remnants of trauma, which I call artifacts, often remain embedded in the subtlest layers of physiology. These artifacts interfere with or weaken the natural healing processes and can corrupt the normal function of other critical systems throughout the body. This can result in the eventual manifestation of illness or dis-ease, both physically, emotionally, and even spiritually.

The Healing Spectrums Sessions create a very high degree of coherence in brain function (see the special brainwave study in the following chapter) and throughout the physiology. This enhanced coherence spontaneously facilitates the release of some of these artifacts. As they are released, the inherent healing processes become even more efficient in their functioning. Certain brainwave frequencies that are known to enliven the body's healing are more quickly activated and expressed during the sessions.

Simultaneously, one experiences a more peaceful and expanded state of awareness that is most often associated with one who has practiced deep meditation for many years. I have had sessions with individuals who had never meditated for even one day of their lives, yet they had this kind of very clear experience during their first session.

Artifacts

The artifacts are simply the emotional remnants of trauma. They are like micro-computer chips of memory that hold the emotional element of the original trauma within the subtlest layers of physiology. These become a subtle part of the foundational neurological function that supports ongoing distress patterns and responses. If we knew they were there then we would all try to find them and attempt to remove them, if possible. The problem is that they are on a very subtle, almost invisible level beyond the conscious thinking mind. They can be so deeply buried within the vast network of physiology that it would be virtually impossible to consciously locate them. This is especially true if we are not aware of the concept of the existence of such artifacts. But even if we were, it would still not be possible to find and release them through any empirical, analytical process.

The Healing Spectrums Sessions gently reveal and release them in a sequence that is totally controlled by the physiology's inherent intelligence. Your body knows best what to do and when to do it, if given the opportunity. My job is to simply make myself available, be present, and observe. That is all I do, without judgment or manipulation. My intention is that it is only for the highest good, as known by the physiological intelligence and underlying consciousness of the individual.

Through that silent witnessing, I am able to view subtle aspects of one's physiology. During that time there are various "spectrums," sometimes violet, blue, green, or gold, and sometimes a blended combination of the spectrums that manifest as a unique quality of coherence within specific areas of the body. I do not and cannot choose which ones should be present. It is just how the "gift" works. It is a very simple and uncomplicated process. I'm glad it is that way because I'm not a complicated person and I greatly appreciate the simplicity!

Energy

I have been asked many times how or if I am "sending" energy. My answer is always that there is nothing to send because there is no space that the underlying life essence does not already exist throughout creation. The idea of sending energy may possibly imply that there is an absence of energy in any given point of creation and that is impossible. However, it is possible that a particular value of energy that exists can naturally and spontaneously become enhanced.

As I found in my own NDE, there is an underlying essence that permeates and unifies every possible particle of existence; like the underlying threads that permeate and appear as a fabric of whole cloth. That essence is manifested as a vibration (frequency) that extends throughout every possible particle of creation, seen and unseen. On the subtlest levels, that which we perceive at any given moment is just a variation of frequency or vibration, all supported and sustained by that all pervasive essence. Ultimately, we are all just "that." Thus, we are living breathing extensions of that eternal underlying energy.

This is why I do not perceive any energy being sent. It is just present without any measurement of time or space. In sessions with people in other parts of the world, there is nowhere "to go" or "to find" a person. We are all infinitely connected... always. It is simply a matter of innocent intention to be present with that uniquely expressed individual. Again, that is just how the gift works.

Who Does the Healing?

People often ask if I am a healer. My answer to that question is always, "I am a healing facilitator. *You* are the healer." In fact, you will never hear me call myself a healer because I am very clear that if there is any healing going on, it is really being done by the person who is being treated. It is their inherent system of healing that is doing the work. My intention from beginning to end is that the session is for the highest good of the mind, body, heart, and soul of the individual. It would be rather presumptuous of me to think it is even possible that I could know what the highest good is for anyone at any given moment. I cannot even know that for myself! However, that information is available within the physiology through the deepest level of the individual's consciousness. It transcends any "thinking" processes that we are generally accustomed to using for analysis or problem solving. So, any healing resulting from a Healing Spectrums Session is truly for the individual's highest good.

CHAPTER 33

ENHANCED BRAINWAVE AND NEUROLOGICAL FUNCTION

"There were significant increases in the unique brainwave frequencies and amplitudes that are known to activate and accelerate the body's natural healing and regenerative processes."

M OST OF US HAVE driven various automobile makes and models in our lifetimes. We generally take for granted that there are certain things we need to know to successfully drive them. We need a key to start the engine, engage the transmission, press the accelerator pedal to move forward or backwards, use the brake pedal for slowing and stopping, etc. We also know there are certain times to bring it in for services, like changing the oil and filters, rotating the tires, and other basic services needed to keep the car running smoothly and, hopefully, to enjoy many years of a smooth driving experience. For most of the cars on the road, we don't even have to read the manual that comes with the car to be able to drive it. We just get in it, start it, and drive.

However, what if someone gave you a super car like a Ferrari, Lamborghini, or some other high-performance car that you had never driven before? Wouldn't it be a good idea to read the manual to understand the unique functions of the car so that you would take good care of it and at least not unknowingly do things that could potentially damage it? You'd probably want to know as much as possible about how to care for it to make it last and perform optimally for many years. So, what about the super high-end vehicles we ride in everyday for a lifetime? Our human bodies. Shouldn't we want to have a basic understanding of how these exquisite rides work and what we can do to enjoy them and make them last for as long as possible? After all, there's no trade-in option!

After going through my own major health crisis and coming so close to permanently leaving this world and this body behind, I was very thankful that I was given a second chance at life. So, I realized that I really should get a better understanding about some of the important functions of this human body. Not that I felt compelled to become a doctor, medical researcher, or any kind of specialized health care professional; I just wanted to know more of the basics that would possibly be in the manual they forgot to give us when we came into this worldly existence. So, I started to do some homework and after the gift of the Healing Spectrums appeared in my life, I was especially curious about the control center: The brain.

After a few years of doing hundreds of Healing Spectrums personal sessions and observing changes taking place during and after those sessions, I became intrigued with the idea of having some initial brainwave studies done. I wanted to see exactly what changes in brainwave function could be happening during the sessions. I had already been learning more about the different brainwaves that serve as the basis of the full range of human function and experience—the how, why, and when they come online to give rise to and support the wide range of physical and emotional human experiences and responses.

As a result of this deep dive into the different brainwave functions, along with all the years of observing the variety of human behavioral patterns, I began to have a sense of which brainwaves were predominantly active at any given moment during the sessions. It was finally time to scientifically verify these changes taking place during the sessions and to validate the efficacy of the sessions. Most importantly, I wanted to be able to explain to healthcare professionals in scientific terms how the Healing Spectrums Method works.

The analysis during initial testing at a university brain research lab clearly showed significant, unique, and immediate changes in brainwave function in subjects while being treated, while treating, while doing the Healing Spectrums Method self-treatments, and during Healing Spectrums Coherence Activations.[23] In every case it was noted that there were multiple intervals of a rapid and major increase in brainwave coherence. There were significant increases in the unique brainwave frequencies and amplitudes that are known to activate and accelerate the body's natural healing and regenerative processes, along with an increased state of emotional well-being.

Increased Alpha

In all cases, we saw a strong and steady Alpha frequency (8-13 Hz) in the frontal cortex. There was little Beta (14-30 Hz) during the Healing Spectrums sessions. Beta is the primary brainwave function mostly present throughout the day for processing information, communication, analysis, and problem solving, etc. Alpha also produces a state of "restful alertness" such as what one might experience in deep silence or meditation. There can be many other health benefits from having more Alpha brainwave function such as reduced stress, anxiety and depression, increased creativity and the ability to more easily absorb new information.

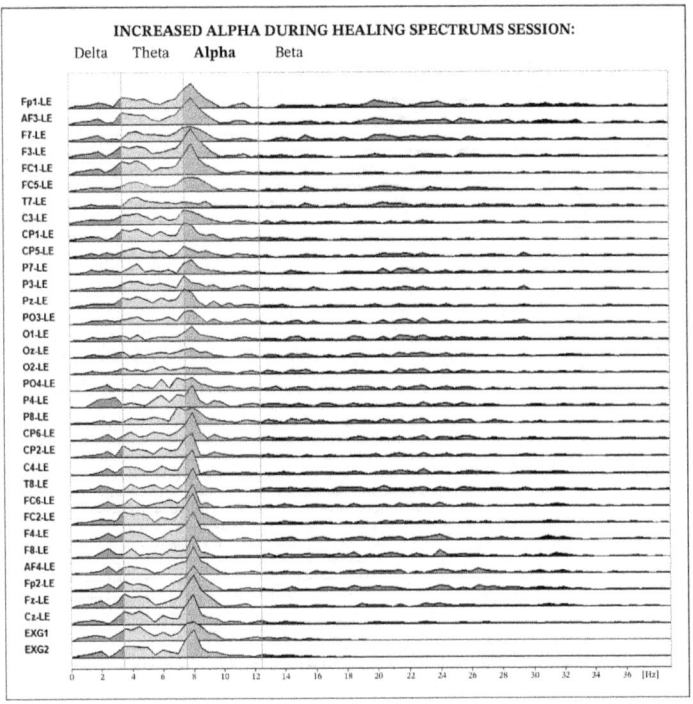

Increased Delta

There were also periods of simultaneous Delta (0.5-4 Hz) frequency.

Delta is the slowest frequency and is often associated with deep stages of sleep. There is generally little to no awareness/no dreaming during sleep at the deepest, slowest stages of Delta. This brainwave frequency triggers deep healing and regeneration, cessation of pain, and enhanced immune response, as well many other positive benefits for both physical and emotional health and well-being.

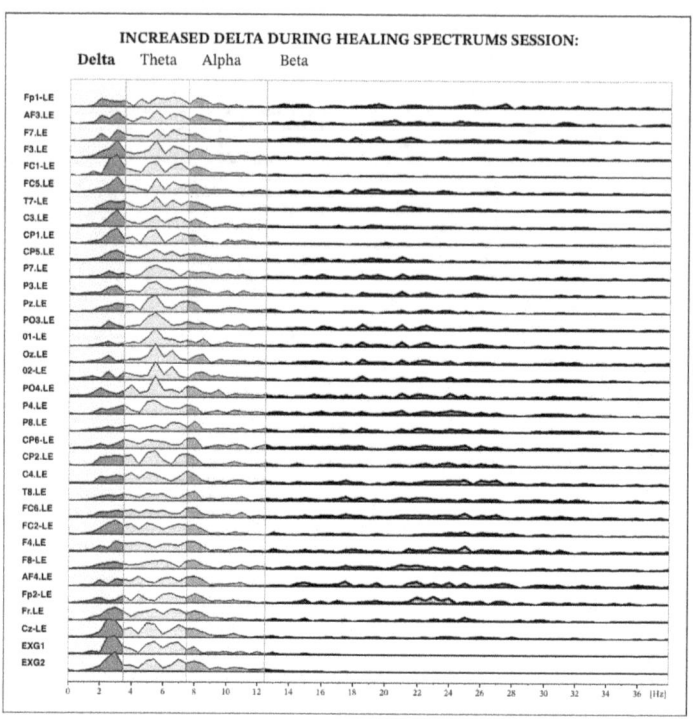

INCREASED DELTA DURING HEALING SPECTRUMS SESSION:

Waking Delta

This is a state of non-thought or "unconscious Delta." I like to refer to it as awareness of awareness only, without any thought or boundaries—a very expansive state of being. It is not actually an unconscious state but more a "super conscious" state of just simple consciousness without thought. (This is the predominant brainwave function of infants' innocent witnessing, until other brainwaves begin to develop around 1-4 years of age and later. Obviously, life outside the womb after a while requires an increasing capacity for learning, analysis, and rational thinking processes which are primarily supported by combinations of other brainwave frequencies.)

Increased Alpha During Coherence Activation

It was also noted that in the moments during the Coherence Activation, provided during Group Healing Spectrums Sessions and when training others how to use the Healing Spectrums Method, there is a massive predominance of Alpha at levels that far exceed even those levels during regular Healing Spectrums sessions or even during some meditation techniques.

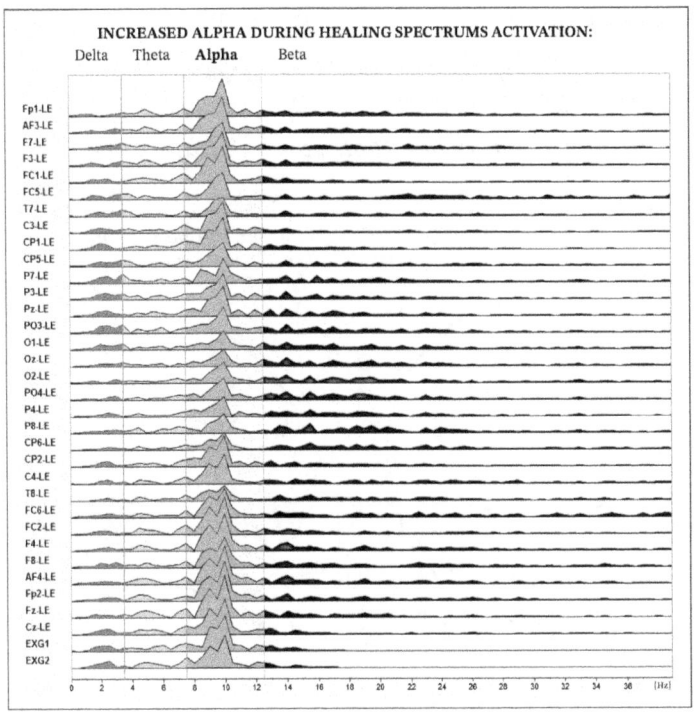

Gamma Frequency: The Brain's Super Processor

There was also an interesting phenomenon in my own brainwave testing while giving Healing Spectrums sessions to test subjects. Gamma (25-100 Hz or higher) is generally not as common as the other brainwave frequencies and is associated with bursts of insight, including spontaneous cognition, and high-level information processing.

This kind of information is not available through any Beta (analytic) process but rather, it is spontaneously accessed via a particular value similar to Waking Delta. Yet, it is on the opposite end of the slow Delta frequency (0.5-4 Hz). *(See examples of this phenomenon in Chapter 34)*

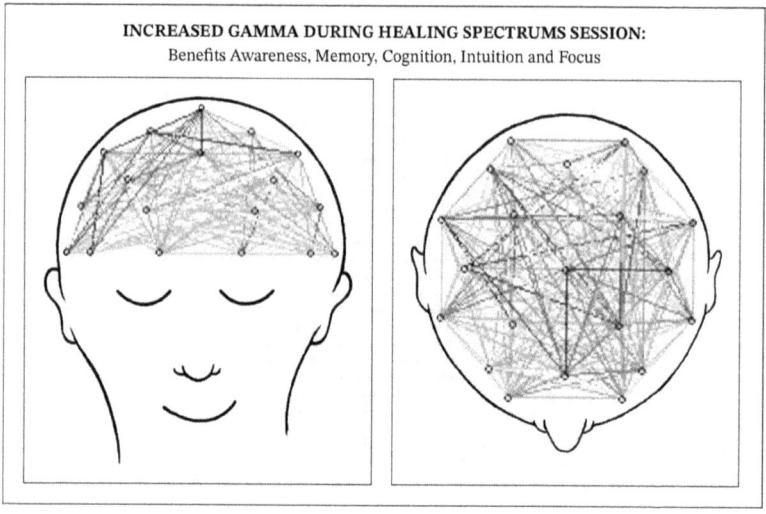

INCREASED GAMMA DURING HEALING SPECTRUMS SESSION:
Benefits Awareness, Memory, Cognition, Intuition and Focus

Additional Benefits of Gamma Brainwaves

- They can improve cognition and problem-solving ability.

- They help with rapid information processing.

- They can improve memory.

- They can help increase attention span.

- They can increase awareness and mindfulness.

- They may boost the brain's immunity and function.

Is One Better Than the Other?

I have encountered a few individuals who like to explore ways to stimulate particular brainwave function, perhaps to enhance unique abilities they feel could improve some aspect of their lives. Some want to be more creative, intuitive, peaceful, psychic, etc. I call this "Boutique Brainwave Manipulation." (That's just my name for it.) I'm not a big fan of this approach, as it may inadvertently produce undesirable results. For example, let's say that one would like to be more creative or perhaps would like to enhance their intuitive abilities. We know that the Theta brainwave frequency is more dominant in those moments of greater creativity and intuition. So, one might logically choose to use a method to artificially stimulate that frequency. However, there is one circumstance where this could produce unforeseen problems. A person with

ADD/ADHD already has a high degree of Theta. Adding more Theta could exacerbate the situation. It would be better for them to seek greater overall brainwave frequency balance.

I do see benefits of using this approach for those who have lost some motor or cognitive function. This methodology has been shown to increase specific brainwave function that can help to create new or alternate neural pathways in the case of damage due to injury or illness, especially in the case of stroke and other traumatic brain injury. More research is being pursued in these areas, including how stimulating specific brainwave frequencies, particularly Gamma, in dementia and Alzheimer patients may potentially be used in the treatment of such cases.

All the brainwaves exist for specific functions human beings need for a balanced life in this world. The brain seeks stasis/balance so there is a unique value and purpose for each brainwave frequency to become more active at any given moment, as needed. No one brainwave is better than any other brainwave. They are all equally important.

Over the years, we have seen many health benefits resulting from the Healing Spectrums Sessions and Programs, including enhanced neurological function and other areas of physical, mental, and emotional health and well-being.

Deep Sleep

While I am not an expert in the field of sleep research, I have spent a good amount of time reading various studies on the topic, especially regarding changes in brainwave activity produced during the various stages of sleep. In fact, it is what led me to pursue having the initial brainwave studies done on the Healing Spectrums Method.

We have all frequently heard about the importance of a "good night's sleep." Deep sleep, that is. It is not so much that we just want to wake up in the morning feeling refreshed. Of course, that is important but more important is whether we had the quality of sleep that effectively activated the body's healing and regenerative processes. Those processes can only occur during specific cycles of the deepest stages of sleep. Research shows why getting to those deep stages of sleep is so important for maintaining ideal physical and emotional health.

Additional research has also indicated that there is a direct link between mental health issues, such as dementia, schizophrenia, and Alzheimer's, and the lack of deep sleep. This is not just regarding how many hours one sleeps but more importantly, whether one is getting enough of that specific frequency and amplitude of "Delta" brainwave function. (During a full 8 hours of sleep, only 25% or less of that time is spent in the deep delta stages and not all at once; that is, if your sleep is uninterrupted!)

Why is this brainwave so important?

Maiken Nedergaard, M.D., D.M.Sc., co-director of the University of Rochester Medical Center (URMC) Center for Translational Neuromedicine says, *"The restorative nature of sleep appears to be the result of the active clearance of the by-products of neural activity that accumulate during wakefulness."*

The Glymphatic System: The Brain's Unique "Catalytic Converter"

When you burn fuel to power your car, it creates corrosive by-products called hydrocarbons, which include carbon monoxide. This is why your car has a system to not only reduce environmental pollution, but also to help to improve the functional efficiency of the machine. This system is called a "catalytic converter."

Likewise, when the brain is burning energy throughout the day, there are corrosive by-products that accumulate within the brain: amyloid beta protein and tau protein. Research has discovered that the brain has its own unique catalytic converter called the Glymphatic System, which helps cleanse the brain and prevent or greatly reduce the residual build-up of these damaging corrosive proteins.

Dr. Nedergaard says: *"The breakdown of the brain's innate clearance system may in fact underlie the pathogenesis of neurodegenerative disorders such as Alzheimer's,*

Parkinson's, and Huntington's disease, in addition to ALS and chronic traumatic encephalopathy (CTE)."

Jeffrey Iliff, Ph.D., a research assistant professor in the Nedergaard lab, says, *"In every organ, waste clearance is as basic an issue as how nutrients are delivered.*

...In essentially all neurodegenerative diseases, including Alzheimer's disease, protein waste accumulates and eventually suffocates and kills the neuronal network of the brain."

He goes on to say, *"If the glymphatic system fails to cleanse the brain as it is meant to, either as a consequence of normal aging, or in response to brain injury, waste may begin to accumulate in the brain. This may be what is happening with amyloid deposits in Alzheimer's disease. Perhaps increasing the activity of the glymphatic system might help prevent amyloid deposition from building up or could offer a new way to clean out buildups of the material in established Alzheimer's disease."*

Activating the Glymphatic System

More research is continually being done regarding potential alternative adjuncts for the treatment of various neurological diseases such as dementia, schizophrenia, Alzheimer's, Parkinson's, Huntington's disease, ALS, and even diabetes, all of which share a common deficiency: the brain's diminished capacity to produce adequate levels of Delta brainwaves. Preliminary university brain lab studies have shown that the Healing Spectrums Method spontaneously enlivens the unique brainwave function that is normally present during the deepest stages of sleep which, in turn, activates and accelerates the body's natural healing processes.

While the Healing Spectrums Method is not meant to replace normal deep sleep, it does quickly enhance the brainwave function that also supports the Glymphatic System. Given that other studies have shown Delta brainwaves tend to diminish by age 40-45 and are virtually non-existent over the age of 75, the Healing Spectrums Method may be able to more consistently enliven and perhaps sustain this all-important natural healing brainwave. There is also research that indicates Gamma Brainwave can activate the Glymphatic System and potentially reduce the amyloid beta protein and tau accumulation in Alzheimer patients. These studies provide hope for developing an effective alternative treatment and therapy for this devastating disease.[242526]

CHAPTER 34

GAMMA: ACCESSING THE INACCESSIBLE

"My brain function is not in a state capable of analyzing or attempting to use any empirical processing during a session. I am in a simple state of witnessing."

IT MAKES SENSE THAT I would periodically produce Gamma brainwave frequencies, as I often spontaneously perceive information that is not arrived at through any empirical thought process, questioning, or analysis during the Healing Spectrums sessions. I often see images, much like photos or short movie clips having to do with the person I am having a session with. I consider these kinds of images to be in the category of artifacts. When this happens, I may not be clear as to the image's meaning. So, after the session ends, I will always share what I perceived and ask if it makes any sense or if they recall any particular experience possibly related to the images.

Release of Fear

One such case involved a woman who had been dealing with an increasing sense of fear and concern for her safety and well-being. At one point in the session, an image appeared of her surrounded by water—big water and very deep. She seemed to be struggling and there was a clear sense of fear. After the session, I asked if this meant anything to her. She seemed shocked that I had just viewed an incident that had happened to her long ago. She described how as a teenager, she was caught in an undertow in the ocean and kept being pulled down. Every time she briefly surfaced, she would be pulled down again. After the third time, just as she realized she was about to die, someone suddenly came to her rescue. This was not something she had even thought of for many years, but she vividly recalled the experience when I shared what I had viewed.

I had a follow-up conversation with her a few months later. She told me that the general sense of fearfulness and concern for her personal safety that she had been experiencing before the session seemed to have completely disappeared. She also had begun to be more involved in various activities that she had avoided for many years. So, the release of that specific underlying artifact had made it possible to be free from the limiting fearful experiences she had been struggling with for some time. It was spontaneously erased from the neuronal network, thus creating a new possibility for renewed joy and ease in her life.

Forgiveness and Healing

I was invited to have one of my Healing Spectrums Group Meetings at a friend's home during one of my many visits to the Chicago area. These meetings were open to clients, Healing Spectrums training graduates, and family and friends who wanted to be treated to the group sessions and learn more about the method and programs. And of course, there was the natural interest in hearing more about my NDE. The meetings lasted about two hours or longer with multiple group sessions interspersed with question-and-answer segments, as well as time for sharing individual experiences resulting from the sessions.

There were about 35 people in a large comfortable space. This was significant in that the larger the group, the greater the collective consciousness, which enhances the coherence within everyone in the room. (That coherence also extends farther out into the environment within the surrounding area.) The enhanced coherence enlivens more rapid and efficacious healing responses for those who are present.

As I went through the first session round, I silently spent a few moments just being present with each person before moving on to the next. I spontaneously viewed some unusual artifacts that revealed themselves in some of the individuals. There was one that really got my attention so after that first session, I shared with her what I had noticed. I had viewed an area inside her chest and saw a very dark and brittle appearance throughout her lungs. When I asked her if she had any bronchial issues, she laughed and said,

"I've had acute emphysema for over ten years." Well, that certainly made sense regarding what I had just viewed!

After that brief discussion and a few others with those whom I had also viewed the presence of artifacts, I did a second session with the group. At the end of that round, I was about to ask for any experiences. I looked over at the woman who had emphysema and she was vigorously waving her hand to get my attention. We were all curious to hear what she had just experienced. She began by saying, "As I was quietly sitting here, I suddenly heard a message that I have to forgive my husband!" I asked, "What do you have to forgive him for?"

She went on to say that he was a smoker and even after her initial diagnosis, he continued to smoke in their home. As her illness progressed, she became more and more angry and resentful over this situation, but he continued to smoke in the home. By the time she attended the Healing Spectrums Group Meeting, her quality of life had been significantly impacted. But even with her advanced condition, she was a very gregarious person and continued to be socially active as much as possible. But this required her to always have a nebulizer nearby.

When she shared the message about forgiving her husband, I asked her if she did. She answered emphatically, "Yes! I forgive him. I know I must forgive him!" Somehow, she felt this may be a necessary part of her healing journey after all the years of being angry with her husband. She knew that she now had to let that go.

There was no doubt that she was sincerely committed in her declaration of forgiveness.

I received a message from her friend the next day. She told me that after the meeting, they went out to a restaurant and enjoyed the rest of the evening. What was interesting to her was the fact that her friend did not have to use her nebulizer, which was unusual. Then a few days later I received another message saying there was an even more unusual experience that indicated to her that something was changing since the meeting. Her friend liked to participate in her church choir. Even though it was a challenge for her, she just didn't want to miss out on being a part of that activity that she had always enjoyed before her illness. However, the other singers couldn't really hear her very well, as she didn't have the lung capacity to project her voice much at all. And she absolutely had to have the nebulizer with her during those times. But this time was different.

The message said that now the others could hear her voice and more importantly, she did not have to use her nebulizer. That had never happened before. So now they were both convinced that this must have had something to do with what happened at the Healing Spectrums Meeting. I was just happy to hear that she was enjoying her life more, for whatever reason.

I then received a letter a month later from the woman herself. She thanked me for having made it possible to attend the Healing Spectrums Meeting and went on to say that she had gone for her monthly checkup with her pulmonologist. After some tests he told her, "Your lung capacity has greatly increased. That's not really possible, considering the long-term damage to your lungs." She asked him if he thought it was a miracle and he said that they don't think in those terms but that somehow her lung capacity increased substantially over the last month. He stated again that this is just not possible so he could not explain it, much less understand it. Of course, she didn't really need an explanation. She was just happy that it happened, and she felt great.

After a few more months had passed, I met her at another Healing Spectrums Meeting. She looked quite vibrant, so I asked her how she was doing since she had sent me the letter. She had continued to enjoy the changes and had not relapsed in any way. She told me she had assumed that it must have been the Healing Spectrums that brought about her improvements. I thought for a moment about that meeting and the moment she suddenly got the message to forgive her husband. I told her that however it happened, I was happy for her, but I believed a lot had to do with the sincere decision to choose forgiveness over continued anger and resentment. And the reason I felt that was because just before the end of that session when she made that declaration of forgiveness, there were two angels that appeared with her and placed their hands on her. I have witnessed this in other cases over the years and it often happens in cases of long-term suffering over issues of loss, grief, anger and resentment. Essentially, not being able to "let go."

The Boot

I had a personal session with a woman in Iowa who was suffering from an intestinal tract disorder. Her ileocecal valve was not functioning properly and was not responding to medical treatment. I began my session as always with the intention that the session be for the highest good of the mind, body, heart, and soul of the individual. At some point in the session, an artifact began to appear exactly in the abdominal area. It was clearly an image of a workman's boot. I did not, as always, question or attempt to analyze what it meant. This is because my brain function is not in a state capable of analyzing or attempting to use any empirical processing during a session. I am simply in a "witnessing" state of awareness. But I knew this image obviously had something to do with some past trauma. After a few moments, it gradually faded and was spontaneously released.

After the session ended, I described what I had witnessed. When I told her it was the image of a workman's boot, she stuttered momentarily and said she knew what that was. She said that her late husband was a violent person who had a drinking problem. Sometimes when he returned from work, he would physically abuse her. During one of those instances, many years ago, he kicked her in the stomach exactly in the area where she was now experiencing the current health issue. She said he was wearing his work boots when he kicked her.

I followed up with her a week later to see how she was doing. She told me that the problem had suddenly cleared up. This is often the case when there is a particular distress in the body. There can be a remnant of trauma, even some trauma that happened in the distant past and maybe has been long forgotten, that can eventually manifest in some kind of pain, illness, or emotional distress. In any case, when this kind of session result happens, I take no credit for it. I know whose body and consciousness is doing the healing. Again, my role as a healing facilitator is simply to innocently witness what is before me and not interfere with the process. That is how the Healing Spectrums gift works.

CHAPTER 35

HEALING SPECTRUMS CASES

"The Healing Spectrums session enlivens specific brainwave coherence that is known to activate and accelerate the body's natural healing processes."

B ELOW ARE JUST A few sample cases of various physical healing responses resulting from the Healing Spectrums Sessions.

Hearing Tom's Tinnitus

Tom had been suffering from tinnitus after years of working in his family's restaurant. The loud clanging of dishes, utensils, and other commonly loud sounds associated with that kind of environment gradually led to his hearing issues. The ringing in his ears continued even when he was not at the restaurant and had become a constant source of agitation and discomfort in his daily life. He would soon be assuming the role of manager, as his parents had decided to retire. This added additional stress, as it would require having to spend even more time in the loud environment that caused and exacerbated the tinnitus.

His friend had participated in a recent Healing Spectrums program and suggested that he have a session with me. I was in Arizona at the time and he was in Chicago, so we made arrangements to have three remote sessions by phone. Shortly after the sessions, he reported that the level of ringing in his ears had considerably diminished. He later wrote to me about his experience: "Hello Thomas. Just thought you might be interested in the results I have experienced regarding the three Personal Sessions we have concluded. As you are aware, I was initially referred to you by a friend as someone that might be able to help with an on-going problem that I had been experiencing, namely tinnitus. I had a constant buzzing and ringing in my right ear that was driving me crazy. I couldn't sleep well, meditate, or just be in a silent room without hearing a constant buzzing or loud ringing. I always had to have a TV or radio on during the day and sleep with a fan on to mask the constant internal noise. Even that really didn't help much. I tried supplements that didn't help and then visited an ENT physician, and they really had no solution other than to refer me to a support group.

Well, apparently our sessions have definitely had an impact. The buzzing has completely subsided and I only occasionally hear any ringing. This is such an amazing relief that it's hard to express. I tried so many other options but I thought I'd be living with this for the rest of my life. It has definitely had an impact in pretty much every area of my life! Thanks again for your continued help and support. I couldn't recommend the sessions highly enough."

Best regards, Tom R., Chicago, IL

Chronic Ear Infections Stopped

Meara studied and trained for many years to become a very skilled classical pianist, but she had struggled with chronic inner ear infections that obviously caused problems in her performance. She had been diagnosed with Mastoiditis, which is a serious infection of the mastoid bone of the skull. Her doctor finally told her that because she already had numerous infections before, it could cause serious, even life-threatening, health complications, including hearing loss, blood clot, meningitis, or a brain abscess if she got another infection. Even just the potential of hearing loss for a musician would be bad enough, but the development of any of these more serious complications would be devastating.

Meara's parents called and asked if I would have a Healing Spectrums Session with her in hopes that it might prevent another infection. I had no previous experience involving this specific kind of issue and therefore, could not say one way or another if it could mitigate future infections. However, I knew that naturally enlivening Meara's own healing and regenerative processes had the potential to help in this situation. So, we proceeded with an initial session. I had no way of knowing if only one session would be enough, but I would have a better sense of that based on what would be presented during the session.

Once I began the session, I observed a predominance of both the violet and the blue spectrums appearing primarily in the right side of Meara's head, ear, and face. The violet spectrum is generally the first to be present, as it brings the initial phase of coherence. It also appears in a wide range of the softer structures of physiology. The blue spectrum almost always has to do with the denser aspects of the body, such as bone, teeth, cartilage and other connective tissue. This naturally made sense to me because we were dealing with both softer inner ear anatomy, as well as bone and skull structure.

It had been requested that I do the session remotely at a time of my choosing. In fact, Meara had agreed to the idea of having a session but for some reason, she didn't want to know exactly when it would take place. Even after the session it was quite some time before I heard of Meara's experience during and after the session. Meara finally reported years later in her own words: "He treated me once and I haven't had another infection since. Well, I didn't even know he was treating me at the time. It was from afar while I was at a friend's house. I found out later from my mom that was what was going on at the time, that he was treating me."

Pain Relief
Foot Pain Relieved

Cheryl was having some trouble with an old ankle injury when she came for her first session. She had initially broken it a few years earlier and had to have a metal plate and screws inserted to hold it together. Over time, she began to feel some general pain and discomfort in the foot. She was about to set an appointment with an orthopedic surgeon to consider the possibility of having the screws and plate removed. However, that was not something she was looking forward to so she decided to have a session with me in hopes that it might help to relieve the pain. I told her that I didn't know if it would, but we knew that the Healing Spectrums Method seemed to provide pain relief for various conditions. It certainly couldn't make matters worse, and the enhanced coherence could possibly activate her own healing processes. I encouraged her to consult with the surgeon if this did not help.

Cheryl responded very well and after a follow-up session, the pain disappeared within a couple of days, never to return. I explained to her that this was the result of her own physiology and consciousness leading the way and that it was nothing specifically that I did through any diagnosis or manipulation on my part.

Back Pain Relieved

There was another interesting benefit that manifested following Cheryl's session. She had not mentioned anything to me at the time of our session about an old back injury that sometimes caused her problems. It happened long ago as a child when she fell out of a swing. She had lived with it well into her 50's, so I suppose she had just accepted that there was not much else she could do about it. She told me about this in her follow-up session because after that session she stopped feeling any discomfort in her back. The remnants of that trauma had disappeared, and she has continued to be pain free for many years. As it turns out, Cheryl just so happens to be one of those rare individuals whose physiology almost instantly responds to the Healing Spectrums, whatever the situation may be.

Kidney Stones
Large Stone Disappeared

David, a graduate of my training program, called me from a hospital room and told me that he had a kidney stone that was too large to pass. The doctors wanted to perform a special procedure to remove the stone. David was not keen on this idea because there are some risks involved in this type of surgery, but the doctors felt there really was no other option. He asked if I could come to the hospital and have a session with him since he had been in a lot of pain. He was hoping for some relief that didn't involve strong pain medication because David was not a fan of having to take any kinds of drugs, if at all possible.

I sat next to his bed and silently did the session as nurses came in and out of the room. He told them exactly what I was doing, and no one seemed to mind. (Nurses are often more open than physicians to the idea of alternative methods, as long as it does not overtly interfere with their work.) David seemed to settle down and even fell asleep after a while. I finished the session and quietly left the room, intending to return the next day.

When I returned, David was sitting up and having lunch. I thought that was a good sign since he didn't have much of an appetite before. I was shocked when he told me that he was preparing to leave the hospital later in the day. I knew they had not performed the surgery yet, so I was quite concerned. When I asked what was going on, he explained that after I had done the session the day before, he felt better and didn't feel any pain. But the doctors were preparing for his surgery and David, being the stubborn person he could be at times, insisted the doctors take another image first. He wondered if the stone was still there, or if it had somehow broken down so that he might have passed it in the night. The doctors told him that he did not pass the stone and that the procedure needed to be done. But he somehow convinced them to take another image and said if it was still there, then fine, he would let them do the procedure.

When the image results came back, they told David that the kidney stone was, indeed, gone. They could not explain it because they insisted that it was simply too big to pass but now it was just gone. I wasn't there for any of those conversations and I was certainly not going to get involved. I would not have been able to convince them anyway that the Healing Spectrums might have had anything to do with it. Besides, it was David's physiology that did whatever it needed to bring about that result. The Healing Spectrums simply provided the coherence that somehow activated his healing and regenerative processes.

(Please note that while the patient received no other medical treatment by the hospital staff—only the Healing Spectrums session was given prior to the scheduled procedure, I make no claims to have cured this medical condition. The Healing Spectrums session enlivens specific brainwave coherence that is known to activate and accelerate the body's natural healing processes.)

Another Large Stone

I received a call from someone about a mutual friend who was dealing with a kidney stone issue very similar to David's recent situation. In fact, that is why I was called because David had told my friend about his experience and that perhaps I could help him. The doctors were not certain whether he could pass this large stone without surgery, but they decided to allow him to return home for a day or two. If it didn't pass, then he should return for the procedure.

When I arrived at Mark's home, I found him lying on a bed and obviously in a great deal of discomfort. In fact, he wasn't even able to stand up without excruciating pain. He hadn't slept or eaten for a couple of days and appeared very weak. I advised him that it seemed likely he may need to return to the hospital sooner than later, especially if nothing improved after our session. (I am very careful to recommend seeing a medical professional in serious cases or if there is any need for specific diagnosis. In other words: I stay in my lane.) I had no idea if the Healing Spectrums would help the stone to pass, but if not, it would at least help mitigate some of the pain.

It was difficult for Mark to settle down at first because the pain cycle had already been well-established by the time I came to see him. However, he gradually became more comfortable and soon fell into a deep sleep that continued throughout the rest of the session. When it was time for me to leave, I quietly left his room so as not to disturb his sleep.

I returned later the next day to check on how he was doing. To my surprise, he was standing and had already enjoyed a nice breakfast. This was certainly encouraging. His pain level had significantly subsided, and he told me that he had slept through the night for the first time since the issue had begun and that he had easily passed the kidney stone with very little discomfort. So once again, kidney stone issues seem to respond well to the coherence provided by the Healing Spectrums Method. There have been other cases involving renal issues where the sessions proved to be beneficial either as an alternative adjunct to regular allopathic treatment or in accelerating post-surgery recovery.

Backs
Back Pain Relief

Walt had been an athlete for much of his life. However, he developed some debilitating back issues over time after he had started a business that required many hours of sitting behind a desk every day. Since I knew that the Healing Spectrums sessions are often very helpful for pain reduction, I offered to have a session with him. As Walt described his experience: "My back had gotten so painful that I could only sit for 20 minutes before having to get up, lie on the floor, and stretch it out. Then I could go for another twenty minutes. This had become my regular routine just to get through each day. After my session, I felt something shift in my back and I completely forgot that I had had any pain at all. I sat for at least another 8 hours working without any back pain or stiffness at all!"

"I Can Run Again!"

Rachael has spinal stenosis and chronic malaise. She could no longer exercise or run and had so much lower back pain she could not walk without debilitating pain. She had also experienced a tightness in her chest and bronchial problems which contributed to her lack of energy and a state of emotional distress. After her first Healing Spectrums session she said she was able to walk much better and the tightness in her chest was way less than before. She said, "I was not at all able to run before the first session. Now I can run again. I feel so much better! I also feel better emotionally overall and I am able to focus much better. I'm very happy and I feel terrific! I love it!"

Knees
Knee Cartilage

It became clear to me that there was some deep distress in Ken's knees where I noticed the brilliant blue spectrums beginning to appear during a Healing Spectrums Group Session. He said that he had briefly felt the pain in his knees intensify and then suddenly it was as if all the pain and discomfort he had been having just poured out through the bottom of his feet. He later told me that the source of his pain was from damaged cartilage in his knees. That was the only time Ken had a session with me.

A few years later, during another visit to Chicago, a man walked up to me and excitedly asked if I remembered him. At first, I did not recognize him. He said, "I'm Ken. I was at one of your group sessions. I was the one with the knee pain." Then I instantly remembered him, but he looked a lot healthier and more vibrant than I recalled. He said the pain was gone after that session and as a result, he also had greatly increased range of motion and flexibility like he had not experienced for many years, all without pain. He had even started playing tennis again.

Sports Injury Healing

A high school basketball player and his mother attended a Healing Spectrums Group Session in Chicago. He had been dealing with a sports injury and had heard the Healing Spectrums might help to speed up his recovery. During the session, I observed the obvious inflammation which naturally appears as a reddish color. That gradually faded as a blue spectrum began to permeate throughout the knee.

After the session, the swelling had significantly diminished and he was able to walk without pain. He later shared his experience: "I had re-aggravated a knee injury from playing basketball the day before Thomas' group session. The knee was swollen and I had to limp when I walked. During the session, I could feel some sensations in the knee and felt the pain steadily easing. After the session, the swelling had all but disappeared and I could walk without pain. Even my mom was surprised when she looked at my knee and saw what had happened. I don't know how it happened, but I was happy that it did! Thanks again, Thomas!" ~ RM, Student, Athlete, Chicago

Shoulders
Deep Muscle and Ligament Rapid Recovery

Even with my understanding of how and why the Healing Spectrums sessions enhance our natural healing processes and having witnessed many cases of rapid recovery resulting from those sessions, I'm still sometimes surprised by the results. I have my own story to share of how the Healing Spectrums helped me make a rapid recovery from a painful shoulder injury.

I had injured my right shoulder a few years ago during a volleyball game and only realized it later that night when I discovered that I could not move my neck, arm, or shoulder without significant pain. It was apparent that

I had a deep muscle and ligament strain in and around the joint. There was obvious swelling which made it very difficult to sleep that night. The next day I called one of my Level-2 graduates and asked for a Healing Spectrums session. He treated me remotely and I also rested and gave myself lots of self-treatments throughout the day and into the night. When I woke up the next morning, much to my surprise, I could move my shoulder and arm with very little pain, had much more range of motion, and I had zero pain in my neck. I would rate this overnight improvement at about 45%.

After one more day of self-treatments there was hardly any pain at all, and my shoulder was back to about 95% of its normal range of function. An injury of this type and severity could normally take two to three weeks or even longer with physical therapy to heal. I felt fortunate to have been treated by a fellow Healing Spectrums practitioner and to have been able to use the self-treatment method for rapid recovery.

Another Shoulder Injury

I ran into Robert at a local coffee shop and I noticed he appeared to be having some issue with his right shoulder. I asked about that and he said he had a skiing accident while vacationing in Colorado and thought he had sprained his shoulder. He had very little mobility at that point and was in constant discomfort, so we arranged to have a Healing Spectrums session before he had to travel again the next day. There was certainly the internal appearance of inflammation during the session but within a few minutes the violet spectrums became present throughout the shoulder. By the end of the session, I did not perceive any of the red hue of inflammation. I told him that if he continued to have pain or mobility issues for more than a couple of days, he should probably seek medical attention, just to make sure not to do any further damage. Regardless of the initial results, I suggested that he give me a call in a few days to let me know how it was going and that we could do another session remotely, if needed.

Robert took off and continued his travels. About two months later, I happened to run into him again at our favorite coffee shop. He said the pain and discomfort had significantly reduced the day after our session. Within two more days there was no more pain and he had regained full mobility in the shoulder. He emphatically promised that if he ever had any issue like that again, he would be sure to call me right away!

CHAPTER 36

HEALING SPECTRUMS SESSION EXPERIENCES

"The self-treatments have helped me in healing some physical issues and I'm sleeping better than ever." - Cheryl Bailey, Counselor, IA

OVER THE YEARS, I have had many friends and clients write in to share their various experiences and results from the Healing Spectrums sessions. Here are just a few.

Healing Spectrums Personal Session Experiences

"After my first session with Thomas, the chronic pain in my knee (cartilage damage) was reduced by 85-90%. My knee completely stopped locking up, and the range of motion dramatically improved. After the second session, the pain was completely gone and has not returned in the three years since my session!" - *Paulette B., Contractor, Chicago, IL*

"I had a bad reaction from inadvertently breathing some vapors from the glue I was using to decorate a costume that I would be wearing in a play a couple of days later. My throat closed down and I could hardly speak. I felt terrible and had no energy. I couldn't imagine how on earth I would be able to perform, as I had many speaking lines to perform. After a session with Thomas, I quickly regained my energy and I was able to perform without difficulty. This really saved the day for me!" *Jesse B, Actor, Fairfield, IA*

"I have had a history of debilitating migraine headaches for many years. I started to feel one coming on and decided to use some of the water Thomas had treated for me with the Healing Spectrums. I placed a small amount on my head and was relieved to find that the head pressure didn't escalate any further. Ordinarily, it would have turned into a full-blown migraine. I don't know how this really works but I'm glad it works for me." *KF, Teacher, Alabama*

"My back had gotten so painful that I could only sit for twenty minutes before having to get up, lie on the floor, and stretch it out. Then I could go for another twenty minutes. This had become my regular routine just to get through each day. After my session, I felt something shift in my back and I completely forgot that I had had any pain at all. I sat for at least another 8 hours working without any back pain or stiffness at all!" *Walt I, Business Owner, Chicago. IL*

"For some time, I had tightness and pain in my shoulders and neck. I used some of the water Thomas had treated on these areas and was pleasantly surprised to find that the pain quickly went away. Now I use the water whenever I feel any tension coming on and I rarely ever have any pain there anymore." *Susan W, Therapist, Iowa City, IA*

"After our session, I felt a smooth, blissful feeling for the next few hours. In general, I continue to feel more settled, grounded and calm and I'm sleeping very deeply now." *Mary, Fairfield, IA*

"The numbness in both hands (Carpal Tunnel) has significantly reduced since my sessions. I also have a deep sense of peace and well-being that I have never known before." *Cindy T, Lab Tech, Iowa*

"I had chronic ankle pain due to working in an auto manufacturing plant and walking on concrete for most of my life. After a long-distance session that actually took place while I was asleep, I woke up and had no pain in my ankles, or anywhere else for that matter. And I was able to enjoy working outdoors all morning with my brother—all without a lick of pain. This really works!" *CF, Mechanic, Lexington, MO*

"I experienced a shift into a profound feeling of peace and well-being during the July10 Healing Spectrums session." *John Ronstadt, Tucson, AZ.*

Healing Spectrums Group Sessions Experiences

"I had re-aggravated a knee injury from playing basketball the day before Thomas' group session. The knee was swollen and I had to limp when I walked. During the session, I could feel some sensations in the knee and felt the pain steadily easing. After the session, the swelling had all but disappeared and I could walk without pain. Even my mom was surprised when she looked at my knee and saw what had happened. I don't know how it happened, but I was happy that it did! Thanks again, Thomas!" *RM, Student, Athlete, Chicago*

"My whole physiology had just shifted, like a wound had healed." *Sue, IA*

"I recently attended a group Healing Spectrums session and all I can say is WOW! I felt an energy flowing all through my spine during the session. I had injured my back during a very bad fall several years earlier. I felt lots of lower back healing all week long after the session and a healing process beginning to bring changes on a fundamental level." *JB, Chicago. IL*

"Prior to joining the remote Group Healing Spectrums Sessions, I had been having a feeling of pain around the area of my heart that had been coming and going for about five years. I felt a release and a sense of deep peace and happiness immediately in the first sessions. After that, the pain just went away. And the next day I woke up and just felt transformed. No pain and no worry." *Sue, Fairfield, IA*

"About a year and a half ago, we signed on for the remote group Healing Spectrums sessions. To our joy and amazement, our pain became more manageable or nonexistent. We took the Self-Treatment Training workshop and have continued with the weekly sessions. This has changed my life." *Jean K, Teacher, Arizona*

Healing Spectrums Level 1 Experiences

"Since beginning the weekly group sessions and the Level-1 Self-Treatment Training, I've noticed that I am more patient and more present. I feel an increased sense of well-being in body and mind and my sensory perceptions are clearer and more pleasing. Oh yes, my sleep is deeper now. In fact, I can hardly remember what it was like before, after only a couple of weeks of the sessions/training." *Richard, Fairfield, IA*

"I took your seminar at the Gateway in Los Angeles just a few months back. I want to let you know that my heel spur is 99% better and that my sinuses have remained clear so far. I have not had any trouble breathing. I also wanted to thank you again for all you did and tell you how much I enjoyed your seminar and the sessions." *Danielle D., Los Angeles, CA*

"I want to thank you again for a most wonderful, amazing workshop this past weekend! I am experiencing a deep integration and wholeness. In some mysterious way, I feel like some blocks have been removed, and the energy in my body and mind has opened up much more. Quite liberating and absolutely amazing!" *Dean A. Los Angeles, CA*

"Absolutely great! Hard to find the words to describe it, really. I find myself smiling a lot when using the Healing Spectrums technique." *Monica F, São Paulo, Brazil*

"I've been doing the Healing Spectrums self-treatment at least three times a day and my body is in a very restful space while I'm feeling and observing the experience.

During the sessions, I noticed some shoulder and hip aches, but they disappeared after the session and I don't have any discomfort there now. I also perceived some subtle colors appearing during sessions: magenta, violet, and finally gold. When the gold is there—wow! It's like nothing else. It's like a rich, molten and deeply satisfying experience. A profound experience! When that happens, there are no boundaries, no time or space, no body. Just a deep awareness of unbounded consciousness. I am loving it!" *Risë K, Cedar Rapids, IA*

"I have been very impressed by the strength of the energy when doing the self-treatments. Last night I was surprised how quickly I went from feeling restless to very relaxed with a short session. Thanks so much!" *Jill P, Oregon*

"The self-treatments have helped me in healing some physical issues and I'm sleeping better than ever. I've also been trained by Thomas to use the Healing Spectrums in my work as a counselor and I seem to be able to 'tune in' more quickly to the core issues of my clients. This is really valuable to both me and my clients." *Cheryl B, Counselor, Fairfield. IA*

"Before the course, I was only sleeping for 2-3 hours a night, but since Thomas' course I'm sleeping unbelievably better! 8-9 hours every night. This technique is a true blessing." *Katherine, Counselor/Coach, NY*

Healing Spectrums Level 2 Experiences

"I feel the knowledge and experience I've gained from Thomas' workshops have given me the ability to significantly help transform people's lives and health. I am amazed at what can happen, even in a short half-hour session." *Ron Schmitz, Fairfield, IA*

"I can't even begin to tell you how much I appreciate how much I learned in your course. My mind is amazed that such a thing as this can happen. Thank you for dying! But we're really glad you came back. Thank you, thank you, thank you!" *Barbara D, Fairfield, IA*

"As a clinical psychologist, I have found the Healing Spectrums Method to be very effective for helping clients to experience relief of symptoms and to become more optimistic, with a greater sense of inner peace and joy. In traditional modes of therapy, it can take weeks or sometimes months to experience such positive results. It is really quite remarkable to have clients achieve these positive feelings early and throughout their therapy process." *Joel Groner, Psy.D, Chicago, IL*

"The energy just gets stronger and stronger. Thank you for sharing it with us." *Susan H, Fairfield, IA*

"Over the years, I have been trained in many different energy and healing modalities, but I have found the Healing Spectrums method to be one of the most powerful of all. Clients often ask, 'Can you do that Healing Spectrums thing?" *Paula B, Chicago. IL*

These are just a few samples of a wide range of individuals' experiences. Sharing the Healing Spectrums through individual private sessions, group sessions, and training workshops has been a constant blessing in my life. I have been continually inspired by the capacity of human beings to experience the unbounded essence of consciousness and to express its vast field of infinite possibilities, as we travel together on this incredible journey.

More Case Histories and Experiences

As of this writing, I have continued to do this work for over two decades and have seen some amazing transformations, physically, emotionally, and spiritually, for countless individuals during that time. There are many case histories and anecdotal reports of the results of the Healing Spectrums Sessions, as well as more information, at thomasgates.com.

After having done individual, group, and training sessions with well over 3,000 individuals over the years, I have been inspired by the amazing ability of the human mind, body, heart, and soul to grow and evolve into higher states of coherent functioning—all for realizing our greatest potential and purpose for being.[27]

QUESTIONS AND ANSWERS

Q: Do you believe in God?

I am always surprised whenever I get asked this question. Perhaps it is because I don't generally use the word "God" in my writings and presentations. I suppose it is more common for people to use the name "God" because that is the most-used name for what I call Source. But whatever we choose to call it, if we are talking about an unmanifest essence that precedes and initiates the first impulse of creation, then I would certainly be fine with the name "God." So why not just say "God?" I have always wanted to make my story accessible to as many individuals as possible and not target any one particular audience. There are many names for "God" and many spiritual paths and faiths. I feel that by referencing that unmanifest essence, commonly known as "God," as Source (with a capital "S"), then perhaps I can reach a broader audience with which to share my journey and whatever benefits it may bring to those readers.

Q: You mentioned the word "stillness." What is your definition of stillness?

I am certainly not a biblical scholar, as I mentioned earlier in my book. However, very much like the first time I heard a professor speaking about a particular quantum particle, I became very excited by the key word in a particular Psalm (45:10) that someone once quoted to me. I really only heard the first line and excitedly declared, once again, "That's right!" That first line is: "Be still and know that I am God." I immediately understood the words, "Be still."

While I am sure that there are many interpretations of exactly what the word "stillness" means, I immediately knew the truth of that word, based on the unbounded journey I had taken in my NDE. A perfect stillness, beyond any thought or any other experience, is the silent catalyst that leads to the threshold of the Source. It transcends what we think or contemplate about God. It is not sitting still in a chair and allowing the mind to roam about with some attempt to know or even possibly hear the voice of God. It is a perfect stillness that transcends all ideals, concepts, theories, or beliefs of how we might come to the pure experience of that God/Source. In that perfect stillness, there is nothing to be attached to that could possibly limit the full, unbounded experience of the absolute finest relative aspect of that which precedes and gives rise to all creation.

Q: Are you a Walk-in?

I had never heard the word "walk-in." So, it took me by surprise the first time I was asked that question. It was explained to me that on a rare occasion during a Near-Death Experience or some other life-interrupting event, a person's departed soul might not return to the body; instead, a different soul could enter that body. I realized why someone might think that is what happened to me because I had no memory of ever having been in this body or even in this world after returning from my death experience.

After being asked the question, I thought about it for a few moments and my answer was, "Would it make any difference if I was? I mean, I'm here and even if I were a walk-in, there would not be much I could do about that anyway!" However, I seriously doubt that I am a walk-in because I gradually began to have memories of various events that had obviously occurred prior to my NDE. But, either way, I am who I am and that's fine with me.

Q: Did anyone speak to you or tell you it was not your time and that you had to go back?

Once I left the body, there was a perfect silence throughout my entire journey. There was an absence of any sound or voices whatsoever. The only time there was any communication from any beings of any sort was in those first few moments after leaving the body when the five beings expressed those soothing words, "Don't worry, everything is alright. We love you. We're here to help you. We love you." Those words were not even spoken, but only silently communicated to me.

Later, just after re-emerging across that invisible threshold from the unmanifest Source, there was a moment when I wondered who was doing this. Who was manifesting my unfolding reality in those moments? There was the unspoken expression, "You are." But there was still a perfect silence throughout the entirety of my joinery. And of course, there was no one to tell me that it was not my time and that I had to return to my body!

Q: Have you ever regretted having to return to this world?

The only momentary regret I had was simply a "mistake of the intellect." It was that very first memory I had in the hospital when I remembered the terrible pain I had endured prior to leaving the body. I was disappointed that I would have to experience that again. However, I was immediately relieved that the pain did not return. Other than for that brief moment, I have never regretted being back in the body and in this world. I had no memories of my life prior to the journey, so I was not attached to any expectations, and I was simply fascinated by where I found myself to be.

I have never been one to have any sense of loss after my NDE. I knew from my journey that there is no "over there." I knew that there must have been a good reason for me to be here and I have never forgotten the eternal essence that permeates every particle of the creation, including myself, that can never be separate from any level of creation. Therefore, I can never lose something that cannot be lost.

Q: What do you say to those who wish they could have a Near-Death Experience?

My immediate response is always, "Be careful what you wish for!" There is a price to pay on many levels, as described in my book. Of course, given what I experienced and how it has changed my life, I would do it all over again if I had to. It provided a life changing view of what this creation truly is and how it works, along with a great appreciation of how fortunate I am to be a part of this world. Having said that, it is important to realize that this is where we grow and evolve as human souls. We have the ability to experience the finest levels of the creation right here. If that were not possible, then everyone would have a Near-Death Experience. I do believe that we must embrace this field of possibility and know that it provides us with the blueprint of how to utilize the vast opportunities the world has to offer to aid us in our journey to Wholeness. That is the Divine Plan.

Q: Why don't the angels communicate with you?

There is probably a good reason they don't. I believe that they are created precisely for very specific roles to help us along our paths to wholeness. They are not bound by the kinds of limitations of perception and intellect that we have as human beings. Thank goodness for that! It is impossible for them to make a mistake. They simply do what they are designed to do. They do not need my input and I trust they know exactly what to do and when to do it, in any given circumstance.

Q: You told the story of witnessing when a new soul emerged during your friend's childbirth. Do you know when a soul enters the body?

That is a question I don't think anyone really has a definitive answer for, other than perhaps the actual soul that is coming in. Some say it is at conception and others say it is at the time of birth and possibly anywhere in between. I've only had the one experience of witnessing the appearance of a new soul just before the actual birth. But I have done many sessions with pregnant clients and have always perceived the soul that is present with the mother, other than that one case. In all other cases, it was like having a session with two individuals. But even in those sessions, I have no idea when those souls first became present. I'm quite sure this question will continue to be debated in religious and philosophical circles for quite some time. I'm just happy when a new soul emerges and has the opportunity to grow and evolve in this diverse field of creation. Again, this is where we come to grow and evolve as souls.

Q: Can you communicate with the deceased?

I cannot communicate with the deceased. I do not intend or request that they may become present. On very rare occasions, I have experienced the presence of an individual's deceased loved one during a Healing Spectrums session or occasionally in other circumstances. (There are some examples in this book.) But when that happens, it is always only to receive a message that is for the person I am having the session with. There is no conversation that takes place. Just a simple message and that message is almost always to let the person know that they are all right, or that they are sorry for any pain they may have caused, and that they simply seek forgiveness. Sometimes it is just a request for the person to let go of their sense of grief, guilt, or remorse, and to move on with their life in a more joyous way.

Having said that, I must also refer to how my own mother made her presence known to me on various occasions in the very early years after her passing. In this case, it was clear to me in each instance that she was there primarily to help me in some way to continue the evolutionary path that was laid before me as a result of the *Journey;* to stay strong, and to simply fulfill my purpose here in this life. After a while, I was no longer aware of her presence. I believe that once she knew I was secure and unwavering in that path, then she simply moved on. I was deeply appreciative of those moments when I felt her presence, but I had no sense of loss once she moved on. In reality, I know we are never separate in this vast creation.

Another important point that is not commonly understood about this phenomenon: Once a person's soul departs from this world, they are moving into a much more refined aspect of creation. It is far less dense than the world they left behind. In fact, it takes a tremendous amount of "spiritual energy" to move in the direction of more density. It is just far less charming to do so. The departed soul always wants to move in the direction of greater expansion with fewer boundaries.

Q: You never call yourself a healer. Why is that?

Indeed, I never let anyone get away with calling me a healer, even when there is any spontaneous healing that takes place. I am a healing facilitator. I simply and innocently observe what is presented before me during a session. I don't analyze, diagnose, or manipulate anything. I function from a witnessing state and my only intention is that the session is for the highest good of the mind, body, heart, and soul of the individual. There is a coherence that spontaneously manifests during the session that enlivens and activates a person's natural healing processes, without my management or direction. This effortless process allows the inherent intelligence of the person's physiology and subtle consciousness to utilize that coherence in the most timely and appropriate way. If anyone says, "Thank you for healing that" or "Thank you for fixing that," I always say, "Thank yourself, because it is your natural healing and regenerative processes that actually get activated to do the work." Also, there are the Healing Angels....

Q: What other healing modalities have you studied and used in your work?

People assume that I must have studied, practiced, or had interest in different healing modalities or systems. While I have occasionally been made aware of other methods of healing, I have not pursued other methods. The Healing Spectrums Method is just a gift that spontaneously manifested sometime after my NDE. I never thought that someday I would do any kind of healing work. I guess you could say that I didn't pursue it. It pursued me.

Q: Why do you do what you do?

As I've mentioned before, I never set out to do any "healing" work but, once it showed up in my life, I knew that it was something that came as a result of my NDE. I was somewhat reluctant to share it at first, because I wasn't sure what people might think. Would they think I was weird or "new-agey?" I wasn't naturally inclined to participate in the more esoteric, New Age ideas and practices I knew many others were into. I guess the most "far out" thing I did was to practice the meditation technique I had learned shortly before my Near-Death Experience. But I knew this was a gift that I would not be able to ignore, so one day I said to myself, "Wait a minute. I died once and made it back. What do I have to be afraid of?" So, I embraced the gift and have never looked back.

While it is certainly fulfilling to know that this gift can help to reduce physical pain, enliven physical healing, and even alleviate emotional trauma, there is an even more compelling reason why I continue to share this gift. It simultaneously enlivens "stillness" and helps individuals to naturally experience the connectedness to that underlying and infinite Source of our existence and that of all the creation. It is always inspiring to witness. Sometimes, that experience alone is enough to change the course of an individual's life in a most profound way.

Q: If there was no one who taught you this Healing Spectrums Method, how is it possible for you to be able to teach it to others?

For the longest time, I had no idea that I would ever be able to teach anyone how to do this. There was no empirical process of learning it. It just spontaneously emerged over time. I always knew that if it was meant for me to someday be able to teach it to others, then it would probably be more about "giving" than teaching. When the "how to" finally revealed itself to me in the "download," then it was quite simple. It was such a special moment when I finally had my first training workshop and experienced the ease of how it all unfolded. I was happy to know that I would not be alone in sharing this gift; that others could also share it and help others benefit from the healing coherence it produces. And not just for the individuals being treated to the Healing Spectrums sessions, but also for the facilitators themselves. Ever since that first training, it has always been consistently effortless and effective. Oh yes, please know that nobody fails! Anyone can do it, even if they have never done anything like this before.

Q: Is the Healing Spectrums Method like Reiki?

The Healing Spectrums is not Reiki. While it may outwardly appear similar, it is different. I have never learned Reiki, but I have trained long-time Reiki masters how to use the Healing Spectrums Method and they have all said that it is different. Each method is effective in its own unique way. My recommendation is always to use whichever method one finds to be most ideal in any particular situation; but it is best not to try to use both simultaneously during a session. This is for the sake of maintaining the integrity and efficacy of the methods.

EMBRACING THE ETERNAL NATURE OF BEING

I N CLOSING, I WOULD like to share with you some final thoughts that I hope you will find to be helpful in your own path to wholeness, beyond the illusion of separateness. I believe applying the lessons of Near-Death Experience can give us a deeper understanding of the true underlying reality of our infinite and eternal existence.

One of the reasons we are drawn to hear more about Near-Death Experiences, or any other spiritual experiences, is that they resonate with the truth that lives within all of us. We came into this world with the innate desire and ability to remember and live the truth of our wholeness. So, it is no wonder that we are enlivened and inspired by listening to or reading about these experiences. However, it is important to realize that it is not the intellectual understanding that moves us to the experience of our wholeness. That alone will not do it for us. If it could, then by now there would not be quite so many bookshelves full of "Spiritual How To" titles! Intellectual understanding is important, but it is only a catalyst with the potential to inspire us to continue pursuing the ultimate fulfillment of our desire. The true experience of wholeness is not something that we can formulate and figure out. It is simply about Being.

So, what are we to do with this understanding? We are all unique in how we can experience that wholeness. We are all highly individualistic human beings with one intrinsic purpose and that is to remember, experience, express, and enjoy our eternal connection to the underlying wholeness of the entire creation, to truly know the Source of our being. Nobody can say that we will all experience this wholeness in the same exact, precise manner. Nobody can tell another what path to take. Each one of us already has the full knowledge deep within of how to remember his or her own wholeness. The main point is that we must have a conscious intention and commitment to fulfill our very purpose for becoming in the first and last place. Consciously living and paying attention to our experiences without straining, as well as naturally enhancing the ability to experience true stillness, will bring the opportunities to us that will show us our own unique paths.

There are many things we can do to enliven the experience of wholeness. Those things are, and must be, up to every individual. Many are drawn to some forms of meditation, particularly those types that do not involve strict or rigid control, while some may choose other methods to help reveal and cultivate their paths to wholeness.

One thing we can be certain of is that wholeness is only experienced in the present. If we find ourselves spending more time in the past or the future, we can take that as a hint that we need to do those things which enable us to be more in the present moment. "Being" is more important than "doing." When we are simply being, then whatever we are doing can gracefully reflect our wholeness in life. Human beings usually turn it around and try to create by doing. We try to control by using the past or the future from which to draw our power and creativity. That is the habit that we are in. It's neither right nor wrong. Of course, we can use the past for analysis and projection, but the real creative juice (impulse) emerges from the present.

It is truly a challenge to trust in the present. We wonder how we can do that. "What will happen? What will happen to me? Will I be taken care of? Can I really trust in the present and be truly safe and powerful?" Those are some of the underlying doubts that we have about it. We all can have, and probably have had at one time or another, the experience of the almost immediate and serendipitous fulfillment of a spontaneous thought or desire: no effort or strain, just complete fulfillment of the intention. It's as if there is some cosmic order-taker sitting and waiting for us to just get out of our own way so it can be given to us! *We* are that order-taker, by way of our eternal connection throughout all creation, including that silent, underlying and unifying Source that is ever-present.

The only thing in the way of our creating effortlessly, spontaneously and powerfully is our own habit of resisting the wholeness that we already are. It is due to the very nature of this highly concentrated and dense physical world that we get overshadowed and forgetful. We often tend to blame people, things, and events for our unhappiness and suffering. That is because we are under the illusion that we are separate from everything and everyone. The highly effective but damaging formula that we have been unknowingly using to resist our wholeness is essentially this: The illusion of separateness leads to judgments of people, places, thoughts or things being good or bad, right or wrong, better or worse, which can ultimately lead to an even greater sense of separateness. It plants the seeds of fear that can lead to anger and ultimately to violence and other stressful events. And it all equals pain and suffering for everyone. But the reality is that we can never be separate from the wholeness of the creation and its Source, because, again, all this manifested creation has its essence in that unmanifest Source.

It is also very important to realize that this day-to-day dense worldly playing field we live within is perfect exactly *because* of its density. Why? Because our own essence and wholeness lies within every single particle of creation, therefore we have a treasure trove of opportunity and possibility to experience and express our wholeness within the density and diversity of this world at any given moment. That may be easier to realize once we leave this world behind. But if we can see it and know it here in this "time zone," then we will have fulfilled our very purpose for becoming.

Now, we can begin to change our habits and embrace the wholeness and the abundance of our creation. All the lessons of Near-Death Experience clearly tell us more about life than death, because as we have seen, there really is no death of our being. It all points to the eternity of life and reassures us of our purpose for being. So, let's enjoy this precious gift of life because that is our birthright. A soul's life is truly eternal and, in that light... nobody dies.

THE DANCE OF CREATION

From a perfect stillness of silence, even beyond all silence,

came the first impulse of creation and in that moment,

the birth of consciousness, closest to its source

and long before its bodily form.

The dance of creation began

from that subtlest impulse, bringing forth

a manifesting essence into form and substance.

Why?

So that unmanifest Source can be divinely expressed and experienced.

The unknown can be known, appreciated, and honored

throughout every possible particle of creation -

from the very first and faintest beginning particle

all the way through the most concrete

and densely manifested forms of creation.

Consciousness is infused with that essence and empowered

to give expression to that which precedes expression.

That is the gift of life. It is our birthright

and our role to play throughout life.

May we always cherish this eternal journey

that ultimately leads us to the realization

of that inseparable Source...

Thomas

ACKNOWLEDGEMENTS

T HERE ARE SO MANY individuals, groups, and organizations who have played unique and special roles in my life that have contributed to making it possible for my full story to finally make its way onto the pages of this book. While it would be impossible to name them all, I would like to express my deepest gratitude for all who not only have been willing to hear my story, but who have also believed in me and continually encouraged me to follow the path that has been laid before me in this life.

Of course, it all begins with my wonderful late parents, Henry and Bobbie Jo Gates. They were always there for me in good times and in challenging times, especially as I went through the biggest crisis of my life. They fully accepted my experience and never questioned or judged how everything had dramatically changed in my life. Not only was their nurturing love and support instrumental in helping me heal and reintegrate into this world, but they also encouraged me to remain strong in my new life purpose.

Thank you, Mother and Daddy, for the honor of having you as my parents.

To my dear sister, Barbara Lovejoy. I honestly believe that I might not be here today if it were not for your timely encouragement and guidance to begin a new spiritual path just days before being rushed to the hospital. I cherish your wisdom and continual encouragement as my beloved sister and mentor.

And to Catherine Gates, who has stood by my side and has been so supportive in my life and my work over the years. In fact, she also recommended to me the publisher of her book, *The Confidence Cornerstone: A Woman's Guide to Fearless Leadership.* Without her unwavering encouragement, it might have taken even longer for my book to finally be completed. Thank goodness she often asked, "Have you submitted your manuscript yet?"

I also greatly appreciate my dear trusted friend, Scott Becker, at StudioArtsPress.Com. From the first time we met, he understood my commitment to share my story and to help as many people as possible to find greater peace and healing. He graciously took on the role of webmaster, content advisor, and graphic designer. His unique artistic talent gives meaningful expression to the most subtle aspects of my story. And special thanks to Scott for the beautiful book cover design!

Many thanks to my cousins, JoLynn Gates and Karen Leabo, for their writing and editing suggestions. I believe that Karen's idea to write my story in a "real-time" format, without interrupting the flow with commentary or interpretation of the events as they unfolded, has allowed readers to move through my journey moment by moment, just as it had presented itself to me. This idea has really helped to make the book much more effective in fulfilling my purpose for writing it.

JoLynn's mastery of the English language, both structurally and grammatically, along with an uncanny eye for those pesky little punctuation gremlins that can sneak in from time to time, certainly helped me throughout the editing process.

Cindi Weeden, much like JoLynn, had an eye for the little writing mistakes I initially missed. She was also a good "sounding board" for clarifying some of the more subtle aspects of the journey. Her questions in that regard were valuable in the writing and editing process.

The mission of my work was made infinitely easier having Lynn Waters as an early partner in sharing my story and workshops across the country. She was great at making contacts and organizing tours, interviews, talks, training workshops, and client sessions, which allowed me to do what I do best. In that way, it has directly contributed to the continuing experiences that have also been an important part of my story here.

My dear friends, Ron and Becky Schmitz, were in the very first Healing Spectrums Training Workshops that I presented to the public. Over the years, they have continued to be amazingly supportive of my work and have also helped in facilitating the training in many of the workshops in Fairfield, Iowa. We have shared so many inspiring experiences of refined perception during our Healing Spectrums sessions together. But my overarching appreciation is for the depth of friendship that we have and how they have continually encouraged me to make this book become a reality.

I'd like to thank John Castagnini, creator and publisher of the *Thank God I... Stories of Inspiration for Every Situation* book series for giving me the opportunity to contribute a condensed version of my journey in Volume 2 of the series. It inspired me to continue writing the more complete story that has culminated here in this book. While it seems we met quite by accident, I realize now, it was meant to be.

Whenever I give presentations or workshops for different groups or organizations on the subject of Near-Death Experience, there are often various notable audience experiences, as well as some of my own, many of which have found their way into my book. One such organization is the Chicago branch of the International Association for Near-Death Studies (IANDS), led by Diane Willis. I appreciate the invitations and opportunities to speak with her groups as, again, there was much that came from those talks that have contributed to parts of this book.

I'd also like to thank Ann Ellis, of the Tulsa IANDS group, for the numerous times she offered to have me speak with her group, as well as provide sessions and training for some of her chapter's members. Ann understands the value of sharing the NDE stories, as she also had her own NDE. She wrote of her experience in her book: *Revelations of Profound Love: New Insights into the Power of Love from Near-Death Experiences.*

Special thanks to Janelle Rowland. Were it not for her insistence that I share my story with her after she observed my sudden and excited outspoken reaction to something the quantum physics professor spoke of that seemed to come right out of my journey, I might not have shared my story with anyone for quite some time, if ever. Until then, I had no idea that there was any reason to share it with anyone. Her reactions to hearing the story showed me why it was important to do so—how it could simply bring healing for others to hear it.

To Betsy Howland and all the good people at Revelations in Fairfield, Iowa for providing the space for many of my presentations and workshops. So many experiences there have contributed to helping bring this book to life.

My old friend, Walt Ingvoldstad, who was instrumental in bringing my work to the Chicago area. Many thanks for providing the opportunity and the space for sharing my story.

And to all my many friends and Healing Spectrums clients, Healing Spectrums training graduates, and practitioners in various health fields: Cheryl Bailey, Sally Henderson, Joel Groner, Vicky Shaw, Jennifer Howland, Stokes Dickins, Deborah Peterson, Paula Battaglio, Jim and Archana Lal Tabak, Haddington O'Heart, Jill Blackwell, Shira Etzion, and many more who have used the Healing Spectrums Method to help their clients and patients over the years. Your anecdotal stories continue to give me inspiration to continue this work and have also provided encouragement to finally complete this book.

And finally, much appreciation for all the good people at Author Academy Elite for providing the guidance and the tools to help me publish my book. It has been a great process that has brought invaluable growth and evolution in my life.

One last note: I know there are far too many individuals I could never thank enough for how they have either directly or indirectly played a role in my life that has led me to bring my story across the finish line. I wish I could name you all, but that would almost be a whole book in itself! Please know how much you all mean to me. Thank you all for playing a part in my continuing journey.

ABOUT THE AUTHOR

Thomas Gates, founder of Healing Spectrums for Health and Wholeness, is a speaker, author, healing facilitator and workshop leader. As a result of his extensive Near-Death Experience many years ago, Thomas discovered that he had an ability to perceive the subtlest layers of physiology and spontaneously enliven individuals' natural healing processes.

He now inspires and empowers audiences throughout the world with his presentations, workshops, training programs, and consultations, as he shares the unique healing gifts and insights that came from his remarkable NDE. Thomas offers personal and group healing sessions and teaches others how to use his simple, yet effective Healing Spectrums Self-Treatment Method. He also trains individuals and health care professionals how to use his programs for the treatment of others, as a complementary adjunct for ideal health and well-being.

Most importantly, it is Thomas' passion to share these experiences with young and old to help them remember and embrace what an amazing gift it is to be a human being—to experience that true, unbounded connection we all have to everything and everyone throughout all of creation, and to use that information to help us enjoy greater health, happiness, and wholeness in our lives.

APPENDICES

How to Change the Habit of Suffering (From the Healing Spectrums Training Program)

A Healing Spectrums Approach

I T WOULD APPEAR THAT stress is a natural part of human existence. After all, there seems to be no lack of opportunity to experience it at particular moments in our daily lives. That doesn't necessarily mean that all stress is bad. In fact, doctors and scientists make a distinction between good and bad stress. An intensely exhilarating experience can actually be stressful on some level of physiology, just as much as one that we consider intensely negative. However, the "good" stress seems to have a less impactful or lasting effect on physiology and can even have some positive benefit. We generally recover from those stresses more quickly than from the "bad" stresses that linger and can cause even more distress. Why is that?

Over the many years of doing thousands of Healing Spectrums sessions, including my own self-treatment sessions, with groups and individuals of various professions and all walks of life, I have had the opportunity to observe the subtle mechanical element of stress and its influence both emotionally and physically. As a result, my view on stress is that it is not necessarily something that comes from the outside and is attacking us or happening to us. Yes, there are environmental challenges we may encounter, physical accidents, and of course, people can say and do the darndest things that can be quite hurtful. But ultimately, the greatest contributing factor to our stress is actually "an inside job."

We often intensify our discomfort internally through the fear of what it means. Have you ever been stressed-out worrying about something because you just know you are right about what it means and just how bad it is? And then, even 5 minutes later, someone may bring new information to you that completely changes the meaning for you and now you are no longer worried but actually relieved? So, what's the difference? There is one common element that is almost always operative in the mechanism of stress. That element is "resistance."

Resistance and fear are running mates, although I believe resistance quite often has its basis in fear. Our physiology is designed to function coherently and will tend to naturally flow in the direction of coherent functioning, given the opportunity. But the more we resist present circumstances or events, the more stress we create and the more difficult it is to find creative solutions that could reduce or relieve that stress. Of course, this is not to say that fear has no redeeming value. A fearful response to a situation that could be life-threatening can trigger an appropriate reaction to avert the danger.

Healing Stress - It's an Inside Job!

Essentially, you could easily substitute the word "resistance" for the word "stress" and begin to get an idea of how stress works and the toll that it can take on mind and body. A very important key to reducing and healing stress is learning how not to resist the fact that it is present at any given moment and to be able to quickly release it so that it does not become firmly established within your physiology's structural functioning.

We may not like or particularly enjoy a stressful experience, but when it comes down to it, it is our creation–at least the experience of how it makes us feel is definitely our creation. I like to say, "Nobody can make us feel any particular way–that's on us!" People can say and do things to us but we ultimately decide what it means. Peoples' mouths move and words come out but how it lands for us is beyond the power of the person who spoke the words or did the deeds. I know, I know–we may want to blame others for how we feel but... It is our resistance to accepting "what is" at any given moment that leads to feelings of stress, fear, anger, sadness, resentfulness, etc. It is a repetitive cycle that has literally become a bad habit.

So, how do we break this habit that causes so much suffering? Well, here's the bad news: You can't *get rid* of a bad habit! It is not just a mental or emotional problem that can be thought, understood, wished, or affirmed away. It is actually a physically entrained habit of function established through neurological, biochemical, circulatory, and endocrine reactions from repetitive stimuli.

But the good news is: You can *replace* a bad habit with a new habit; one that is more to your liking and that serves you better. So instead of resisting the old one, we can create and embrace a new one that brings with it new possibilities. After a while, the old habit seems to fade away as the new one becomes more established. What is actually happening behind the scenes is a process of neurological entrainment that is supported by the brain's neuroplasticity.

And now this leads us to the next section that will introduce a simple but effective tool that will help to replace the habitual stress cycle and create a new habit leading to greater mental and emotional well-being.

Shortcuts to Wholeness: How to Change the Habit of Suffering

It is one thing to have a technique such as the Healing Spectrums Method or other methods that can help to release some of the accumulated stresses that we pick up and store along the way in our lives. It is another matter of if and how we re-train ourselves not to store so much of it in the first place. Of course, it is likely that we *will* have our fair share of trauma or stressful experiences. Stuff happens!

Fortunately, there is an underlying alarm system built into our physiology that lets us know when we are about to go down the "rabbit hole" of a stress cycle. However, unlike a home or car alarm system that we immediately respond to, we typically don't recognize this alarm when it gets activated. It actually works extremely well, like clockwork, but since we were never told of its existence, much less how to use it, we continually fall victim to the "habit of suffering." Actually, I think it should be taught at a very early age and we could skip a lot of unnecessary suffering in life! What is this quick and easy to use shortcut that can change the habit of suffering and how do we use it?

Below is the basic outline of the *Shortcuts to Wholeness* that will give you a very clear understanding of the *Illusion of Separateness* and how to use this simple technique for quickly cultivating and nourishing a new habit that can change the old habit of suffering. This will, in turn, create experiences of greater wholeness and well-being.

The Cost of the Illusion of Separateness

As human beings, we have all picked up a very debilitating habit. It sabotages the fulfillment of our very purpose of being. I simply call it the *Habit of Suffering* or the *Illusion of Separateness.* It is at the very basis of all suffering in life and yet, we don't even realize when and how we are doing it, but we always get the same results over and over again. One thing for certain is that we have become masters of perpetuating this habit and we often unknowingly support it in others throughout society. But the evolution of world consciousness is always calling out for us to change this pattern.

As we have noted in earlier chapters of this book, it is not possible that anything in the entire field of creation can ever be separate. There are only different expressed values of the underlying Source permeating all creation. So there must be something happening that causes us to experience suffering in the first place. That something is a decision, based on a simple *Illusion of Separateness* that takes place almost beyond any logical or conscious thinking level. Once that decision has been made, the physiology, which actually produces and supports the emotions, will activate the necessary processes that result in the experience of suffering.

An analogy I like to use is this: When you go to a restaurant and decide on something from the menu, the waiter or waitress then takes the order back to the kitchen. The chef begins mixing all the various ingredients needed to prepare your meal. After a while, your completed order is then placed before you. All you did was place the order but you did not witness all the ingredients and various processes taking place in the kitchen. This is very much the way a trigger works that sets off some repetitive emotional distress pattern. The trigger is the "order" that gets sent and the physiology is the "chef" which activates its recipe and then masterfully produces the emotional response. Of course, you would not consciously choose to repeatedly place an order for something you already know you really don't like. It's simply an unconscious, underlying, neurologically entrained response that becomes activated by some event, words, thoughts, sounds, etc., that serve as the "trigger." It's important to note that this is the same process that takes place to produce emotions of happiness, as well. The chef has an almost unlimited number of recipes and is always on call, ready to fulfill your order.

Interrupting the Cycle

As was mentioned earlier, it is almost impossible to get rid of a bad habit. Resisting it won't change it. Trying to talk ourselves out of it won't work, either. Once it has become neurologically entrained, it is very difficult to unwind through any analytical process or affirmation. It has become part of the overall physiology. But we can change it first by interrupting its cycle at a critical moment each time this habit is triggered so that it can gradually be replaced by a newly introduced habit, ideally a healthier and more positive one that does not cause suffering. Here is another simple analogy to illustrate this point:

Let's say that you are incredibly good at shooting basketball hoops. In fact, you are so good at it that you simply never miss! The ball goes into the hoop every time you release it from your hand. Swish! You could hit the net without even looking at it. That's how good you are at this. The ball just automatically goes into the net, every time. It is a successfully acquired habit that was established by lots of practice so that it is now fully automatic. But what might interrupt that consistent outcome?

Now, let's say that I am standing next to you. When you shoot your ball, we know that it is going to go right into the net, as usual. However, I decide to shoot a ball after you have released yours and my ball hits yours just as it is about to go into the net. This causes your ball to miss the net! What just happened? My ball interrupted the cycle (habit) of the usual outcome. It created the "possibility" of a different outcome other than what always happens. This is actually how the *Shortcuts to Wholeness* technique works. It simply interrupts the cycle at a key moment and creates the possibility of a different outcome. Just as the repetitive emotional distress patterns were created through neurological entrainment, new and healthier emotional patterns are created the same way.

So here is the technique!

1. **Recognize that there is an underlying habit that always leads to suffering and know who is responsible for that habit.**

   a. There is a response that gets triggered by something that happens, by something that someone says, or by something you see, smell, taste, etc. Most of the time you don't even know what happened that triggered the response.

   b. In actuality, your response or how you choose to define what happened has nothing to do with the person or thing, or event. That's just something that happened.

   c. You are the only one who can say what it means. You are the only one who can make yourself feel any particular way because it is your physiology that is producing the effects that you feel. The emotional response is produced through physiology. It is the kitchen where the chef takes the order, mixes the ingredients, and prepares the meal to fulfill the order.

d. The tendency is often to blame someone else and make them responsible, but it is ultimately your responsibility. It is your physiology that produces the emotions you feel.

2. **Understand the mechanics of how this habit is created and how it works.**

a. Stimulus + Reaction = Emotional Response.

Something from your past gets triggered and brings up a response that is more appropriate for handling that past experience, but not so appropriate for the present experience. In other words, the response is not nearly as effective as one fully based only on the present experience, without the attachments to the past.

b. So now you are not fully experiencing the present and therefore cannot most effectively respond to the experience in the most appropriate and creative way. The creative energy is overshadowed by the energy spent on resisting whatever is occurring at the time.

3. **Introduce a simple, quick, and effective technique**

One that will change this habit and bring greater health, happiness, and wholeness in life.

Here is the standard (long) version:

A. Stimulus with some physical sensation.

B. Stop!

C. Ask yourself: "What do I feel?" Not what you *think* about what you feel... Just find where in your body you feel some sensation, tightness, restriction or discomfort.

D. Simply notice where it is in your body and acknowledge that, without any thought or analysis of what it means.

E. Then ask yourself, "What is the judgment?"

F. DO NOT THINK! This is very important! Odd to ask something and not think about an answer, isn't it? But it is critical not to start analyzing. It is not about what he, she said, or any judgments assigning blame, etc...

G. THERE IS ONLY ONE ANSWER HERE! If you get any other answer, you are not actually using this technique. You are doing what you always have done before that brings the same old results.

THE ANSWER: "Oh, I'm just saying that I'm separate again, that's all."

H. Then just let go and experience whatever comes next. All you are doing is briefly interrupting the cycle or the physiologically entrained response pattern. This may be just enough to spontaneously bring about the possibility of a different outcome. Of course, you may still get the same results as before, at least in the initial stages of using this technique. But after a short while, you should begin to have some very surprising results.

The Short Version:

When it's too late to use the long version. All hell breaks loose and you're in the soup! What do you do now?

A. Stop!

B. Yell out inside: "What time is it?"

C. Don't look at your watch!

D. Answer: "It's now!"

E. Then just let go and experience whatever comes next. Again, all you are doing is interrupting the cycle. Also, when you yell out to yourself, even if silently, you really want to get your attention—like if you were walking with a friend who was not paying attention and was just about to step into the street with oncoming traffic. You would make absolutely certain to get his or her attention. That is how you want to shout out to yourself at that moment. You might even shout out loud so that you actually hear your own voice. Although, I don't recommend this if you are out in public. You might bring even more stress into the situation!

Commit yourself to easily create this new habit.

The habit to always respond in a repetitive way when triggered by certain circumstances is very well-entrained. So if you don't establish a new habit, nothing will change.

Enjoy the benefits!

Believe it or not, it is actually one of the most incredibly simple things to do! But that's just it; it is so simple that at first, it is not as easy as it may seem. Because the old habit is so deeply entrained, you will soon forget to take the action for change and not make the change, unless you are truly committed to sticking with it for at least one month or longer, as needed. If you do this, I can guarantee that you will suffer less and you will be much happier in your life. There will be far less resistance to the fulfillment of your intentions and purpose in life.

I have often heard back from individuals who have taken this to heart and used it. Many have said that it has changed their lives. Whenever I hear this, I always ask, "How could such a simple thing change your life?" Their answer has always been, "I don't sweat the small stuff anymore. I'm just a lot happier." Many have also said that after a while, they don't even have to go through the steps of the technique anymore. They just seem to quickly realize that they have a choice: "To suffer or not to suffer." It has become an automatic choice to choose the latter. So go for it. Give it a try and see if it can help you reduce the stress in your life and enjoy greater peace and happiness.

Healing Spectrums Sessions and Training Programs

Thomas offers a variety of Healing Spectrums Programs, including personal sessions, consultations, and training workshops. Visit www.thomasgates.com for details.

Healing Spectrums for Health and Wholeness Programs

Healing Spectrums Coherence Activation Sessions

The Live-Streaming Healing Spectrums Coherence Activations provide a simple, scientifically verifiable way to spontaneously activate and accelerate your body's natural physical and emotional healing processes.

Personal Healing Spectrums Sessions with Follow-up Consultation

These individual Healing Spectrums sessions provide the opportunity to have one-on-one personal sessions with Thomas. With the unique increased brainwave coherence spontaneously created during the sessions, the body's inherent intelligence and healing processes are effectively enlivened and greatly accelerated.

Sessions are available in-person or remotely.

Healing Spectrums Enhanced Emotional Healing Sessions

These advanced personal sessions are uniquely designed to help release the underlying, habitual neurological/physiological patterns that support and sustain long-term repetitive emotional distress. This method can also be used for accelerated healing from more recent traumatic events.

Sessions are available in-person or remotely.

Level-1 Healing Spectrums Method Training - Learn the Self-Treatment Method

Learn how to use the simple but effective 5–10-minute Healing Spectrums Self-Treatment Method to effortlessly and spontaneously activate and accelerate your body's natural healing processes. These individual one-on-one online training sessions are provided through easy live streaming.

In-person or Online training available.

Level-2 Healing Spectrums Method Training - Learn to Treat Others

Advanced training for individuals from all walks of life to use the Healing Spectrums for enlivening individuals' natural healing and regenerative processes.

In-person or Online training available.

Level-2 Healing Spectrums Method Training - Advanced Training for Healthcare Professionals

Advanced training for physicians, nurses, chiropractors, physical therapists, acupuncturists, and other healing facilitators. Learn how to integrate and use this unique method in your practice as an alternative adjunct for accelerated healing.

In-person or Online training available.

Enhanced Emotional Healing Method Training Program - For Mental Healthcare Professionals

Advanced training for counselors and therapists. Learn how to integrate and use this unique method in your practice as an alternative adjunct method for accelerated emotional healing.

In-person or Online training available.

ENDNOTES

1. **Mom and Dad:** The irony in this experience is that my mother, who was the gentle, quiet spiritual force in my life, happened to be about one hundred miles away in another hospital. She was recovering from a non-life-threatening surgery that had been previously scheduled just before my emergency surgery occurred. Even though she could not physically be there with me, I felt as if she were near throughout my ordeal. Mother and I always had a subtle telepathic connection that could surprise me at times. Sometimes she could suddenly walk up to me and answer a question that I was only just thinking about asking. Other times, when I'd make an unscheduled phone call to her before the days of caller ID, she'd answer with, "Hi Tommy, how are you?" even before I had the chance to say anything. So, it's not surprising that she let her subtle presence be known to me at this time of crisis. It was comforting to have my father physically there with me, but Mother was clearly there in her own special way.

2. **Gaps:** This is regarding my recall of experiencing the "Life Review." It was the one experience of my entire journey that I had no memory of having—until many years later. When I did remember it, it was not like a "memory." It was the full experience, as if it were happening to me for the first time, all these years later! It was truly a powerful and humbling experience.

3. **More Gaps:** Much later, after returning home from the hospital, I remembered having this experience and realized that I had viewed my own death from a previous life. It might explain why, even as a child, I never really liked trains. It's not just that I didn't like them. I was always agitated by the sound of metal grinding on the tracks, and I simply found everything about them to be somewhat irritating and disturbing. I had little interest in them, and I usually avoided them. However, after this unusual experience in the hospital, I gradually became more comfortable around trains and I have since taken a few trips on them, which I found to be quite enjoyable.

4. **Point of Departure**: I know where that point is on every person now. Many years later after my experience, I was sharing my story with someone who asked if I could show her exactly where it was located on her head. Without thinking, I spontaneously touched her head. She suddenly inhaled deeply, and her head quickly snapped back. I was able to help her regain her balance and then asked what had just happened. She said she felt herself rushing up to the spot where I had touched her. After witnessing such an unusual reaction, I thought that I should probably be more careful with that. I'm not sure that it could happen, but I would not want someone to pop out and possibly leave his or her body, even if only temporarily and especially if permanently. I could only imagine trying to explain that!

5. **Divine Beings**: Guru Dev was the one who was initially responsible for the revival of the meditation technique that had so inspired me only a few days before the emergency surgery. I didn't know much about him at all, only that he had been a powerful inspiration to many throughout India. He was honored and respected as a humble but great enlightened spiritual leader of his time who also brought millions together during World War II to meditate and pray for peace and enlightenment for all. Over the years, I have continued to notice the essence of Guru Dev and even Jesus and the healing angels in my life, particularly whenever I am sharing my story with others and especially while engaged in the sharing of the healing gifts that resulted from my death experience.

6. **The Light**: Most individuals who have gone through a Near-Death Experience have reported seeing a white light at the end of a tunnel and that they are naturally drawn to it. There have been a few reports of those who, for some reason, chose not to go towards the light and instead chose to go elsewhere. I believe it is still one's choice to choose but I recommend to simply "let go" and go to the light. It's usually an automatic response and it will prove to be quite a pleasant experience.

7. **NDE Reference?** When I went through my experience, I had never heard of Near-Death Experience before. There were no books or discussions readily available regarding this topic. Raymond Moody's first research book on this topic, *Life After Life: The Investigation of a Phenomenon—Survival of Bodily Death* was released three years after my experience; therefore, I had no preconceived ideas about it. In the very beginning moments of my journey, I had simply surrendered to it as it naturally unfolded, moment by moment, without any expectation to see anyone or anything in particular. I believe that if I had begun with a strong desire or belief that I would meet someone, perhaps Jesus or family, or that I might see Heaven or any other number of possibilities, then this golden light might have been the most likely pathway for that to happen. Although no one appeared to vocally speak to me during my experience of the golden light, I have since learned that it is not an uncommon experience for many individuals to meet previously deceased family members, Jesus, or other beings in the "Light" during their own NDE.

8. **Quantum Physics and the Particle:** Years later, when I first described this experience, I learned that quantum physicists theorized, even though they are not yet able to "see" it, that this is one of the initial and most elemental building blocks of physical creation. I suppose it could either be the first or the last particle, depending on which direction one's consciousness is moving at the time it appears! (More on this in Part 2)

9. **Source or God?** I have often been asked, "Do you believe in God?" That is a question that always surprises me when I share my story. The answer to that is: I believed in God long before my NDE. Even as a child, observing the magical flow of nature while spending so much time alone in the woods, I knew there had to be something that made it possible for all this to exist. The truth of that was as obvious to me then as it is now. So, when asked, if by Source I mean God, my answer to that is this: If God would be the originating source and catalyst of all creation, then I'd agree Source is, indeed, God. My hope and purpose in sharing anything at all about my journey has always been to help others remember their infinite connection throughout the entire creation by the eternal grace of God—that underlying true Source of all that exists. That truly is our birthright. My goal is to share this with as many as possible, no matter how they can hear it. Whether the word God or Source can fall upon their ears, I also believe that everyone has that connection, whether they consciously remember it or not. It is part of the DNA of consciousness, even if only at the subtlest level of awareness. That spark exists in all; otherwise, there would be no point in creation at all. There is learned knowledge and belief. Then there is the experience. The experience is what we all truly desire, far more valuable and enlightening than any intellectual, philosophical, or religious doctrine. That is all well and good. It has its place in our pursuit of enlightenment, but by itself, cannot provide the actual experience we seek.

10. **The Illusion of Separateness:** Later, in Part 2, I will explain how the Illusion of Separateness causes us to forget the truth of our existence and opens the door to human suffering. At the end of the book, I will share a simple method for how we can change the habit of suffering so that we may experience more joy and wholeness in our lives.

11. **Gone for How Long?** My journey had begun after the doctor's announcement to my father that I might not make it. It all took place in a space of time after they had left the room and before they had later returned. No one knows how much time had actually passed. Although, to me it seemed like an eternity, I believe it all had taken place in only a matter of moments, if not minutes.

12. **Good to Be Alive!** That was the last time I ever felt any sadness about being in my body. Since that time, I have never, ever wanted to be anywhere else but right here and right now, fully present in this body. I ultimately realized that this is the place to be! It was no accident that I am here. I know that I was meant to be here, even though there was no one at any time who said, "It's not your time. You must go back." I realized that I am truly here for a purpose. Otherwise, I would not have returned! Why bother? Why take on the unknown, ever-changing, and uncertain possibilities that can manifest in a human being's lifetime? There can certainly be many bumps and bruises along the way! Existing as a human being provides the most dense, concrete expression of consciousness. This is where we have the greatest opportunity to experience the full range and purpose of our being. Even through the difficult experiences in life, there is always the possibility for growth, gratitude, and evolution. If we can experience the truth of our wholeness in this most densely created space of existence, then we will have mastered and fulfilled our complete and true purpose for being. We will experience the full range of our divine existence throughout every possible particle of creation and, therefore, know that we are not separate from anything, anyone, or any moment in all of creation. We then consciously walk with that clear essence of God Source always within our lives.

13. **No Place Like the Present**: This has continued throughout my life. I am not nostalgic regarding my past. I get much more pleasure from the present as it unfolds and I am not naturally inclined to hold onto past events, whether joyful, terrific, sad, painful, etc. I suppose I generally find the adventure of the moment to be much more interesting than something that has already happened. Of course, I know that it can be beneficial to revisit a past memory that can elicit some feeling or emotion, but it can never be the same feeling or emotion that happened in the actual moment of the initial experience. Besides, we are constantly changed by our experiences and are not the same as when we first had our past experiences. Often, letting go of the past can potentially allow us to experience new possibilities for even greater growth, expansion, and fulfillment in life, trusting in the moment.

14. **The Thread**: That faint blue translucent thread was the same as I had previously experienced during my journey—the one that was connected all the way back to my father's heart after I had left the body and continued to move into a deepening unbounded experience.

15. **Witnessing**: This was just another example of that subtle coherence that underlies everything in the creation and interconnects us all. And it is true: Music is the universal language of love and connection. It can bring us together in the most profound way that can transcend all the apparent chaos that sometimes distracts us from the truth of our connectedness to one another and to the entire creation.

16. **Divine Presence**: This experience also proved to be the first of a few experiences I would have over the years with the presence of Jesus and various Healing Angels as I continued to share my story during my travels across the country.

17. **Interference**: I found out much later that it was not an uncommon experience for many people who had Near-Death Experiences to have these kinds of issues around electronic devices. I even knew a fellow musician who had been in a bad motorcycle accident and went through his own NDE. After his rehabilitation, he discovered that he could no longer play electronic keyboards. Every time he touched one it instantly stopped working! He always had to be sure to add in his performance contracts that he could only play on an acoustic instrument. I also met a woman who, after her NDE, could not touch any electronic kitchen devices: blenders, mixers, toasters, digitally controlled ovens, etc. They just instantly stopped working. She got her fair share of friendly jokes that it was a good excuse to keep her out of the kitchen! But I know she would have preferred not to have that issue.

18. **Indecision**: This was a challenging process that I have witnessed many families go through. It is understandable that we want to have the presence of our loved ones in our lives for as long as possible and we want to feel that we have done everything we possibly can to have them stay with us. We also have our different beliefs and philosophies about the ultimate reality of life that sometimes collide with one another in such difficult moments of facing the imminent passing of a loved one. Even though we know death is a part of life, it is never easy to let go. I hope anything I have shared here can be reassuring that in the end, the one who is in the process of passing ultimately will know exactly what to do in those subtlest moments as they begin their new journey. Again, in the end, there is no ending....

19. **NDE or Death?** It still feels odd to think of it as "near." As a friend who also went through it once said, "Near? There ain't no near about it!"

20. **Challenges of Spiritual Evolution**: As a matter of fact, any individual working through their own spiritual evolution, even those who have not experienced a NDE in this lifetime, will be challenged to stay within the "box" of society's and family and friends' expectations for them, of how they used to be. It is so important to maintain authenticity through all spiritual evolution and change, accepting change and expansion, and knowing that relationships and friendships are likely to change, and that's ok. Everyone's evolutionary journey is entirely unique and personal. It is important to accept and love others for who they are while always remaining true to one's own spiritual path, sometimes even "moving on" if necessary.

21. **IANDS**: International Association for Near-Death Studies (IANDS) www.iands.org. This organization has existed for over 40 years and is a wonderful resource for both experiencers and family and friends who seek to learn more about the NDE. Here, you can find other stories of experiencers, researchers, speakers and so much more.

22. **Wings?** I have never seen wings when viewing any of the angels. They can be anywhere at any time in an instant. So, it would seem that there really is no practical need for wings. But perhaps they might serve another purpose, unknown to me.

23. **Healing Spectrums Brainwave Study**: The initial brainwave studies were done at the Maharishi International University Center for Brain, Consciousness and Cognition, Fairfield, IA. A baseline mapping of cognitive and response times was established via computer testing of each subject prior to being treated by the Healing Spectrums practitioners/facilitators. Practitioners/facilitators were also given the baseline testing prior to performing the Healing Spectrums sessions. Before and after brainwave function was then analyzed and compared to establish changes and the efficacy of the Healing Spectrums sessions.

24. **Gamma Brainwave Research**: Gamma Oscillations in Alzheimer's Disease (AD) and Their Potential Therapeutic Role: Artemis Traikapi and Nikos Konstantinou - Department of Rehabilitation Sciences, Faculty of Health Sciences, Cyprus University of Technology, Limassol, Cyprus **Sensory Gamma Frequency Stimulation in Alzheimer's Disease Patients:** https://www.frontiersin.org/articles/10.3389/fnsys.2021.782399/full

25. "The accumulating evidence on gamma entrainment through visual and auditory stimulation in mice was a major stride toward establishing the importance of gamma brain waves, particularly at 40 Hz, in the amelioration of AD neuropathology. The research on the therapeutic efficacy of gamma sensory stimulation in AD patients, although still in its infancy, provides encouraging data. Clements-Cortes et al. (2016) evaluated the effects of 40 Hz sound stimulation vs. non-rhythmic visual stimulation in AD patients. The study indicated that somatosensory stimulation, *via* a device (i.e., NextWave chair) which produced 40 Hz sound waves through six speakers, had a significant effect on the cognitive function of patients with mild to moderate AD, in contrast with the visual stimulation which involved nature pictures displayed on a television screen. While patients' gamma brain activity or possible changes on AD pathology were not assessed, this study provided solid evidence regarding the efficacy of gamma-based treatment in AD. – continued...

26. ...More recently, Suk et al. (2020) developed a light and noise delivery device and stimulated at 40 Hz cognitively healthy, AD, and epileptic patients while their electrophysiological responses were recorded. The concurrent audiovisual stimulation was proved safe in all subject groups, including the epileptic patients, while induced highly coordinated 40 Hz oscillations. Even though patients' cognitive abilities were not examined, this study provided preliminary evidence regarding the safety and feasibility of 40 Hz sensory stimulation in AD patients.To investigate the efficacy of sensory stimulation as a novel disease modifying therapy in AD patients, Chan et al. (2021) conducted a longitudinal, placebo-controlled trial. Specifically, 15 patients with mild AD were recruited and divided into experimental and control groups. Both groups were given the same sensory stimulation device to use at home for 1 hour daily. The device was programmed to deliver constant white light and noise to the control group and synchronized audiovisual stimulation at 40 Hz to the active group. AD patients who received real auditory and visual stimulation treatment daily, over a period of 3 months, presented reduced loss of functional connectivity, improved memory performance and ameliorated sleep markers in relation to controls. Additionally, the active group showed less brain atrophy and more importantly did not show further hippocampal atrophy or ventricular expansion in relation to the control group, indicating a possible delay in the disease progression. In the same manner, He et al. (2021) recruited 10 patients with prodromal AD who received daily 40 Hz audiovisual sensory stimulation for 1 hour over the course of 4 or 8 weeks. Even though control group or sham stimuli were not included for comparison reasons, the study indicated that the treatment was safe and resulted in improved functional connectivity in the default mode network and altered cytokines and immune factors in the cerebrospinal fluid. Overall, both studies provided compelling evidence that gamma-based therapy, through visual and auditory stimulation, may have a disease modifying effect and may be used to alleviate AD pathology. Table 1 summarizes the clinical studies that applied gamma frequency brain stimulation in AD patients."

27. **Complementary Adjunct:** As an effective alternative/complementary adjunct to traditional health care, the Healing Spectrums sessions and programs are not a substitute for treatments ordinarily administered by health care professionals for physiological or psychological conditions. While there are medical doctors and licensed health care providers who use the Healing Spectrums Method as a complementary adjunct in their practices, neither Thomas nor any associates or representatives of the Healing Spectrums for Health and Wholeness Programs make any claims to treat or cure any illnesses or diseases.